Build a Better Trade Show Image

Build a Better Trade Show Image

By Marlys K. Arnold, ImageSpecialist

**Tiffany
Harbor**
Productions

Chapters 14 and 16 were originally written as articles for the Trade Show Exhibitors Association's *Trade Show Ideas* © 2000, 2001. Reprinted with permission of TSEA.

Exhibitor statistics included are from Exhibit Surveys Inc., the Center for Exhibition Industry Research, EXHIBITOR Magazine, Tradeshow Week magazine, the Gale Group, and the Exhibit Designers & Producers Association. Reprinted with permission.

Excerpts from *The Experience Economy: Work is Theatre and Every Business a Stage,* © 1999 by B. Joseph Pine II and James H. Gilmore, used with permission of Harvard Business School Publishing.

This book contains various trademarked names, which are used for editorial purposes only and benefit the trademark owner with no intention of infringing on the trademark.

Unattributed sidebar quotations are by Marlys Arnold.

Cover art and photo by Alan Arnold. Interior illustrations by Laura J. McCormick.

First printing 2002

Publisher's Cataloging-in-Publication
(Provided by Quality Books, Inc.)

Arnold, Marlys K.
    Build a better trade show image : establishing brand
by designing a dynamic exhibit experience / by Marlys K.
Arnold. -- 1st ed.
    p. cm.
    Includes bibliographical references and index.
    ISBN 0-9712905-1-2

    1. Trade shows. 2. Marketing   I. Title

T396.A76 2002   659.1'52
                       QBI01-201329

Dedication

To my husband Alan,
  This book truly would not exist without you.
  Thanks for always believing in me, keeping me
  on track, and scheduling all those "brain dates"!
To my parents, Howard & Wynona Haun,
  I've never been known for following the usual path.
  Thanks for always giving your support and for
  encouraging me to do my own thing.
To my teachers,
  While many will say they always knew I'd
  write a book some day, a few helped make
  it happen. Thanks to Helen Beckham,
  Joe Hinz and Bev (Olson) Buller for teaching
  me a love for words; to Mary Anne (Siefkes)
  McCloud for teaching me how to be a good
  reporter; and to Professor Ruth McCreery
  for challenging me to write my very best.

Contents at a Glance

Table of Contents

Foreword

We are in the midst of a trade show and event revolution. Never before has brand and image become as important as it is today in the exhibition industry. Branding is so key in today's trade shows that corporations are moving responsiblity from the product side of the house to the marketing communications side. Traditional show floors are rapidly migrating from product showcases to branding environments; invigorating settings where attendees experience the brand through sight, sound, touch and feel.

This change has brought a whole new breed of trade show and event managers to the forefront. In the past, inheritors of successful exhibit programs often rested on the program's past laurels. Today's exhibit managers must seek new ways to invigorate the minds of attendees though interactive branding environments. Every aspect of the trade show must be totally integrated to achieve true success. So you are probably asking yourself, where can I go to get the knowledge to become a successful exhibit manager in today's world?

Look no further! You are about to embark on a journey that is a must-read for everyone in the industry, from the corporate exhibitor to service suppliers. In this book, Marlys Arnold creates a great parallel between the steps you would take to build your ideal house and those necessary to create the perfect trade show image for your company on the show floor.

Most books about trade shows to date have focused only on one or two pieces of the show. Now there is a book that focuses on the integration of all the elements necessary to create and execute a successful trade show exhibit.

If you take time to read only one book about executing a successful trade show or event and thereby building a better trade show image for your company, make this the one!

- E. Allen Reichard,
Vice President of Corporate Exhibitor Programs,
The Freeman Companies

Acknowledgements

It would be impossible to thank all the individuals who helped make this book possible. It is the result of hundreds of conversations over the years with exhibitors, show organizers and industry suppliers. Thanks to all who so willingly shared their experiences.

While countless people contributed to this book, a few have really gone above and beyond to help see it into print. Special thanks to Penny Ripple, David Mihalik, Kathy Sudeikis and Allen Reichard for their numerous phone calls and e-mails to answer my questions.

Many thanks to the following people for granting permission to use statistics or excerpts from their work: Trade Show Ideas Magazine, EXHIBITOR Magazine, the Exhibit Designers & Producers Association, Tradeshow Week magazine, Joseph Pine and James Gilmore (authors of *The Experience Economy*), the Gale Group, Exhibit Surveys, and the Center for Exhibition Industry Research.

Special thanks to my editors: Katie Gibson, Alex Kolker and Brian Bailey. You make me look good.

I would also like to thank Laura McCormick for designing all the icons you see throughout the book (as well as on the web site).

Introduction to the Building Process

"Brand awareness." "Generating buzz." "Experiential marketing."

Everybody's talking about these popular business topics today, but how many trade show exhibitors are really putting them into practice?

Although trade shows have existed since the days of the Medieval fairs in Europe or the traveling caravans in Arabia, it's easy to see that today's shows are far more complex. It's no longer about simply showing your wares and closing a sale on the spot with a slick sales pitch. Today, the focus has shifted to using your exhibit as a three-dimensional marketing tool to create and define your unique brand – a living personality for your company.

Attention spans have become increasingly shorter. Generations X and Y (which now number about 100 million) have grown up in the age of media and are used to thinking in sound bites and video clips. They're looking for instant gratification. They want a total experience that's interactive and invokes all of the senses. And if you really want to impress the "MTV generation," you must create an experience that is cutting-edge and fun, as well as educational.

On the other hand, our high-tech world needs personalization. Show organizers have been fearing the onslaught of virtual shows, yet traditional trade shows continue to thrive and many convention centers are expanding. Why? It's because computers and technology cannot replace the physical experience and contact at a hosted event. Business is built on personal relationships between individuals.

So how does an exhibitor or show manager hope to compete in this "brave new world"?

First, you must think of the exhibit as an extension of your overall integrated marketing plan. When done right, a trade show encompasses nearly all other marketing tools: direct mail, advertising, incentives and promotions, sponsorship, sampling, telemarketing, public relations, and that elusive word-of-mouth (also known as "buzz").

"Products today are becoming commodities; extremely similar and easy to clone, with similar pricing," says Allen Reichard of The Freeman Companies. "Exhibitors must look to branding to differentiate how they are perceived. The old mentality just won't cut it anymore – you can't keep [exhibiting] the same old way."

Companies should strive to constantly reinvent themselves, much like Madonna has done to stay at the top of the music business. If you take pride in doing things the same way you've always done, you may soon find yourself left in the dust.

In this book, you will discover how to develop a complete marketing plan for your exhibit, which includes setting goals, figuring return on your investment, and all the stages in between. You'll learn from exhibitors who are thinking "out of the box" to create unique exhibit experiences that distinguish their company and brand. You'll also follow the progress of two fictional companies as they use the information in this book to develop their own exhibiting plan.

This is the book that I wish I could have found when I first began exhibiting. Now, I've collected stories from my years spent as an exhibitor and attendee, as well as a show organizer, in order to share what I've learned with others. I'm an optimist – every time I go to a show, I expect to see exhibitors who rise above average. Unfortunately, those exhibitors are still very much the minority.

My challenge to you? Don't just read this book. Take the examples and use them as a springboard for your next creative session. Start thinking in a whole new way. It's just like building a house; you don't want to live in a neighborhood where all the houses look exactly alike, do you? Make yours unique and watch the way people respond. You may find that you are a trendsetter!

Now, let's start building your new trade show image!

- Marlys K. Arnold

How to Use this Book

No matter what your level of experience in the world of trade shows, this book has tools for you.

It is organized into six sections that focus on each aspect of trade show planning. These sections also follow the analogy of building a house.

Throughout the book, you will see special elements, such as a flashlight or file cabinet. Here is a key to these symbols:

 "Rule of Thumb": statistics, survey results or other things to remember

 "Bright Ideas": tips and examples from other exhibitors

 Vocabulary: you'll know if a word is listed when you see it's underlined, "linking" it to the vocabulary section at the end of that chapter

 Resources: at the end of each chapter and in the back of the book

At the end of most chapters, you will be able to follow an ongoing exhibit plan for two fictional companies. Each chapter builds on the previous ones, so look for these symbols to read the new section for that chapter.

You won't find any photos in this book, but you will find photos of some of the examples online. Because the trade show industry is constantly changing, this book will be updated on the Web.
Whenever you see this symbol,
you'll know there's more
information or images online.
Just log on to:
www.imagespecialist.com/build.html
to view photos and find out what's new.

You will also see reprints and excerpts from my monthly online column called TradeShowTips Online. You may also sign up for these monthly trade show tips on the Web site.

Your opinions and comments about this book are always welcome! Please feel free to send an e-mail to marnold@imagespecialist.com or mail to the address listed in the back of the book. Be sure to include your name, address, and phone number or e-mail address. I would also love to hear about any successful ideas you've used in your exhibiting, whether they were sparked by this book or not. You may just find your story on the Web or in a future edition of the book!

Although numerous resources are listed in the text and resource guide, you're not obligated to use any of them. Take some time to investigate your options before hiring any supplier.

Please note that I cannot answer every question related to the topics in this book. Due to the high volume of mail received, I may not be able to reply to every message.

Disclaimer

This book contains information gathered from many sources. It is intended to provide general information about the subject matter covered. Although the author used diligence in the writing and made every effort to ensure accuracy, we assume no responsibility for any errors, inaccuracies, omissions or inconsistencies. Any slights of people, places, books or organizations are unintentional.

Neither the author, publisher, distributor nor retailer is engaged in rendering legal, psychological or accounting advice. None of the above shall be held liable in the event of incidental or consequential problems in connection with the use of ideas contained in this book. For specific advice geared to your individual situation, consult an expert in your area. No book can substitute for a personalized consultation.

Breaking Ground Before You Begin to Build

You wouldn't start building a house before you surveyed the land and drew up blueprints, would you?

Why then do so many trade show exhibitors skip this important step when they decide to exhibit at a show? In fact, how many exhibitors fully research the show before they even sign the contract?

When you start a major project, it's always better if you put some thought into it before jumping in. Remember the old carpenters' adage: "Measure twice, cut once." While you may be tempted to skip straight to the chapter on booth design or promotions, resist the temptation! You'll be much wiser making those kinds of decisions if you've started at the beginning, which means first you must ...

Survey the Land

Did you know?

➡ Less than 25% of exhibitors set goals for their exhibits. And of course, many who set goals don't actually follow through with them. So it's no great surprise that so many exhibitors are dissatisfied with their show results. But by following the advice in this chapter, you'll put yourself ahead of the crowd and avoid major disappointment.

Before you even think about signing a contract with show management, first ask yourself:
1) Why am I exhibiting?
2) Who are my targets?
3) What do I want to accomplish?

Did you answer Question 1 with any of the following?
- Because we always exhibit there
- Because my competitors will be there
- Because it would look bad if we weren't there

Sorry! None of these are valid reasons! Does that surprise you?

Instead of going to a show just because it seems like the right thing to do, you must truly evaluate how it fits with your overall marketing plan and budget. (If it doesn't fit, then you might as well stay home.) For example, ask yourself if you want to:
- gain qualified leads
- introduce new products
- conduct market research

When you fail to plan, you might as well plan to fail.

Old carpenters' adage: "Measure twice, cut once."

- gain media exposure or publicity
- enhance your company image
- meet power buyers
- provide samples or demos of your product to prospects
- educate clients, prospects or dealers
- spend quality time with existing customers
- shorten the sales process/make on-the-spot sales
- enhance word-of-mouth reputation
- open doors for sales reps in the field

Goals must be:

↦ Measurable

↦ Realistic

↦ Communicated to the entire staff

These are more concrete goals, which can be clearly communicated to every member of your exhibit staff in order to get them all working toward the same objective. These goals can also be quantified. It's not enough just to determine goals – there must be a way to measure them. Only then can you truly look back after the show, evaluate the return on your investment (ROI) and justify whether or not to return to the same show next year. Measurable goals must have a number attached to them. Don't just say you want "a bunch of leads." How many is that? Instead set goals like:
- gain 100 qualified leads
- receive attention in 6 media outlets
- generate $10,000 in on-the-spot sales
- hand out 500 samples

While some of the goals in the first list don't lend themselves to a specific number, that doesn't mean that they're not good goals. You just need to know how to recognize if you've been successful. For example, opening doors for future sales calls could mean that you book appointments with prospects there at the show, or that you track sales calls over the next six months and see how many came as a result of people visiting your booth.

Be sure your goals are realistic and attainable.

TradeShowTips Online
Issue #13: "Why Exhibitors Fail"

So many times I hear exhibitors grumbling that a particular show was a disaster. They blame show management for not doing enough to bring in the traffic. Yet they don't seem to realize they have the ability to help turn that situation around themselves!

Why then do so many exhibitors fail?
- Failing to set goals (or else setting unrealistic ones). This is probably the biggest reason. If you don't have a goal, how will you know if you've had a successful show or not?
- Assuming that people will magically show up. Yes, show management is responsible for getting people to the show. But how will they find your booth in the corner? Invite them!
- Sending a staff that hasn't been properly trained. You wouldn't turn your teenager loose with the family car without a single driving lesson, would you? Then don't turn your staff loose on the show floor without some basic education.
- Being arrogant! Arrogance comes from being a know-it-all who needs no planning or training because "we've done this for 20 years." Just because you've done it before doesn't mean you can't do it better this time.
- Making assumptions. Another kind of arrogance comes from judging people negatively by their looks or name badge. Assume everyone has potential – remember, even if they aren't the final buyer, chances are they will be able to recommend you!
- Frightening attendees! The opposite of the arrogant booth staffer, these staffers are so desperate that they attack everyone in the aisles and send them scurrying away.
- Over pitching instead of listening. Yes, you need to let them know about your products and services. But more important, you need to listen to them. Find out their needs, whether or not they are in the market for what you do, and if they are a qualified buyer.

Once you've learned to avoid these common mistakes, you'll never sympathize with all the exhibitors around you who are complaining about what a rotten show it was!

Why They Go

The Center for Exhibition Industry Research (CEIR) has discovered that some of the more popular reasons people have for attending shows include:
- gather competitive intelligence (the #1 reason people attend)
- generate ideas and plan for future projects
- gain "hands-on" experience with products
- see new products
- talk with experts
- study industry trends
- examine products first-hand and comparison shop
- acquire personal development and training
- network

(Source: CEIR Report #AC33)

Why don't they attend?
- nothing new to see
- poor service from booth staff previously
- wasted their time last year

(Don't set a goal of 1,500 leads if only 2,000 people will attend the show!) If goals are unrealistic, it will actually de-motivate your staff.

Did you know?

- The average <u>consumer show</u> attendee spends 3.6 hours at the show and only spends significant time in three to five exhibits.
- The average <u>trade show</u> attendee spends 9.6 hours (over two days) on the show floor and visits about 20 to 25 exhibits (averaging 23 minutes per visit). *(Source: CEIR Report #AC27B and AC/RR 1090.)*
- Almost 70% make a purchase decision as a result of attending a trade show exhibition. *(Source: CEIR Report #AC/RR 1100.)*
- 88% have not been called on by one of your sales representatives in the past 12 months. *(Source: Exhibit Surveys Inc.)*

Now, on to the question: "Who are my targets?" Did you answer, "Everyone"? Guess again! No product, no matter how wonderful or unique, will reach every attendee at a show. So how do you go about figuring out how many of the attendees are realistic prospects?

Exhibit Surveys Inc. has developed a formula that you can use to answer this question. Not only will it help you in setting your goals, but also in determining how much booth space you will need in order to handle the expected traffic. (More on this in Chapter 6: Generate Energy.)

Formula for Determining Leads Goal

A = Total show attendance

B = Number of highly interested prospects (The industry average is that 16 percent of attendees come to a show interested in any specific type of product; this can be higher in very specialized shows.)

AIF = <u>Audience Interest Factor</u> (How many of the prospects are likely to stop at your booth? The average for a general interest or consumer show is 25 to 30 percent. For a more specialized trade show it can be 50 percent or more. The national average for all shows is 48 percent.)

C = Total number of potential leads (this number should be your goal)

> "If you don't know where you're going, you'll probably wind up in the middle of nowhere."
>
> – Anonymous

	Net Attendance	A
x	% of Audience interested in your type of product = # Highly Interested	x .16 ——— B
x	% who will likely stop (AIF) = Total Potential Leads	x .48 ——— C

(Source: Exhibit Surveys Inc., CEIR Report #MC1)

Now, to make it even more manageable, take your Total Number of Leads (C) and break it down by hour. (Divide your number of Potential Leads by the number of hours that the show is open.)

The chart on the following page shows two examples: a general interest (<u>horizontal</u>) show with an estimated attendance of 5,000, and a more specialized (<u>vertical</u>) show with 2,000 attendees expected. The chart shows that even though the general interest show has a much higher attendance, there really isn't much difference in the total number of leads generated because the audience is more highly qualified.

(American Slide Chart designed a Trade Show Activity Planner that exhibitors can use to estimate staffing and promotional material needs. See the Resource list on the following page.)

Exhibiting at a show has many benefits. It's a rare occasion where the buyer actually comes to you – and on neutral territory – providing you an opportunity to build a relationship. This is more cost-effective than field sales, because you can see more people in a shorter amount of time and also shorten the sales cycle. And perhaps the biggest benefit is that you can sell in 3-D: prospects see, hear, touch and interact with your products.

OK ... so now you know why you're going to a show and what you're hoping to gain from it. Now the next step is to decide which shows will be the best match for you.

> "Whatever you think a project will take, double it. That goes for both time and money."
>
> – Anonymous

Comparison Study of Two Possible Shows

	Total Show Att.	Qualified Prospects (16% of att.)	Audience Interest Factor (AIF)	Leads Goal	Total Show Hours	Leads Per Hour
General Interest Show	5,000	800	30.00%	240	16	15
Special- ized Show	2,000	320	52.00%	166.4	16	10.4

Vocabulary

Horizontal show: has a broad range; audience is very diverse

Vertical show: targets a particular niche market; the more vertical the show, the higher the audience quality, but the competition is also much tighter among exhibitors

Public/Consumer show: a show that is open to the general public

Trade/Industry show: a show that is open only to qualified members of a specific industry; the term "trade show" is loosely applied to describe all types of exhibitions

Association show: a show that is held for members of a particular association, often in conjunction with the annual convention

AIF: audience interest factor; the percent of attendees that visit at least two out of 10 exhibits in a category; the national average is 48 percent

ROI: return on investment; calculating how much business was generated compared to the amount of money spent on the exhibit

Sales cycle: the process that begins with a basic lead and ends with that lead becoming a customer

Resources

American Slide Chart (planner)
800-323-4433
www.spinslidepop.com

Center for Exhibition Industry Research (CEIR)
312-808-2347
www.ceir.org

Exhibit Surveys Inc.
732-741-3170
www.exhibitsurveys.com

Fictional Case Study: DigiCrayon

Scenario:

A small educational software company who wants to showcase their newest creation: a landscape design program, featuring an online gardening guide

Show:

Local Home & Garden Show, estimated 20,000 attendees over three days (28 hours); a horizontal consumer show

Exhibit:

10' x 10' booth

Goals:

Out of those who stop at the booth:
- Sell 250 software packages ($49.95 retail at a show special of $35; $8,750 total sales)
- Gather mailing list of 500 names
- Gain local media coverage (at least 2 stories)

Breakdown:

18 leads and 9 sales per hour

Fictional Case Study: Purple Carrot Press

Scenario:

A children's book publisher wants to showcase their new line of collateral materials (stuffed toys, games, puzzles); two main characters to feature: Sunny the Frog and Alyssa

Show:

Regional book and toy retailers' show with an estimated 7,000 attendees over two days (14 hours); a vertical trade show

Exhibit:

20' x 30' island booth

Goals:

Out of those who stop at the booth:
- Gain 550 leads (stores to possibly carry products)
- Sign up 100 new retailers within 30 days of show
- Gain media coverage (at least one TV and one print)

Breakdown:

40 leads per hour

"The future
belongs
to those who
prepare for it."

– Ralph Waldo
Emerson

Select a Site

Did you know?

➥ There are 13,185 shows held each year in the United States and Canada. *(Source: CEIR 2001 Exhibit Industry Census)*

➥ It costs an average of $233 to gain a lead at a trade show, versus $302 per lead in the sales field. *(Source: CEIR Report #SM17)*

➥ Companies spend 17 to 21% of their marketing budget on exhibitions. *(Source: CEIR Power of Exhibitions II)*

Just because there's a big show coming up in your industry doesn't mean you have to exhibit. Does that shock you?

Before deciding to exhibit at any show, do your homework. Start by studying trends in your industry and checking with related associations and trade publications for shows that they participate in. Do an online search at TSNN.com or TradeshowWeek.com to search by industry, location or show date. Once you've developed a list of possible shows, talk with each show manager and ask the following questions (many of these may be answered in the exhibitor prospectus):

1. Who attends and why?

This question is more about audience demographics than total numbers (think quality, not quantity). What kind of information is collected on the registration form? The best information is available when a show has been audited, which means the numbers have been verified by an

> The worst reason to exhibit is because you think your absence will be noticed!

We don't hesitate to ask for advice from friends on everything from books to read to restaurants to try, so why not do the same thing for trade shows to exhibit in?

independent, unbiased third party, such as ABC Expomark. Audits are taken from a census-based statistical sample (not survey-based projections), much like the ratings for other forms of media (Nielson, Arbitron, etc.). Audited information can help to justify your participation in the show as well as proving ROI, according to Expomark's Paula Fauth. An audit will not only tell you the total number of attendees, but can give a demographic profile of those attendees, including:

- the number of verified attendees (both paid and unpaid)
- the number of exhibit personnel
- analysis by business category and job title
- analysis by geographic region

Remember: Your success is based on how well attendees fit your target demographic profile! (For more information on audits, check the Resource Guide on page 21.)

2. Is there an admission charge? If so, how much?

This can affect attendance. With a small fee, more people may attend, but with a larger fee, it may weed out all but the most serious buyers.

3. Where will the show be held?

Find out if it will be in a location convenient to you, or perhaps in a geographic area you want to target. Keep in mind that, even with "national" shows, the majority of attendees will always come from the region where the show is being held. If it is the kind of show that moves around from year to year, you may want to wait until it comes closer to you. Also, your overall costs can be significantly different for a show in Memphis, Tennessee, versus a show in New York City. Factor this into your decision.

Average Daily Cost for Select Major Cities

	Lodging Costs	Total Daily Costs
Atlanta	$112.00	$242.74
Baltimore	$97.00	$214.24
Chicago	$190.00	$311.89
Cleveland	$105.00	$213.44
Dallas	$188.00	$294.09
Denver	$112.00	$227.54
Detroit	$99.00	$204.60
Kansas City	$113.00	$204.59
Las Vegas	$97.00	$185.94
Los Angeles	$178.00	$298.99
Memphis	$114.00	$227.64
Nashville	$102.00	$203.84
New Orleans	$177.00	$273.77
New York City	$237.00	$408.14
Orlando	$126.00	$227.19
Philadelphia	$154.00	$265.09
Phoenix	$129.00	$232.74
San Francisco	$204.00	$318.44
Seattle	$117.00	$250.69
Washington D.C.	$184.00	$323.44

*Total Daily Cost includes meals, ground
transportation, hotel and other
incidental expenses.
(Source: Corporate Travel Index,
Business Travel News)*

4. How long will the show be open?

Knowing this will help you determine how much your booth will cost per hour (booth space rental divided by the number of hours of the show). Remember, even if the fee sounds reasonable, a six-hour show may not be worth all the time, energy and money it will cost you. On the other hand, if it's a highly targeted market full of big-ticket buyers, it could prove to be worth the expense. Another question to ask, if the show is part of a convention, would be how many of the exhibit hours are "show only" (not competing with seminars and other events).

5. What other exhibitors will be there?

Ask if you can get contact names for previous exhibitors and call non-competing companies to find out their experiences. They can also give you insights on audience demographics, whether show management is helpful, and if they felt the show was a worthwhile investment. Keep in mind, however, that most of these names referred by show management will be those who they know are favorable. (That's simply smart marketing on their part!) If you really want an objective opinion, ask for a copy of last year's show directory. Then you can select a handful of companies to call (at least eight or ten), including some small exhibitors who were in less than desirable locations. If they had a positive experience and plan to return, that's definitely a good sign!

Another possible resource for information is to interview is the show's decorator or general service contractor (GSC). They may hear things that exhibitors never tell show management,

> Know that if you're a first-time exhibitor, chances are you won't be able to reserve a prime booth space. Booth assignments are often made on a priority point system, meaning that long-time exhibitors will often get the preferred locations.

Working a Show Without a Booth

Even if you can't have an exhibit in a big show, you can still take advantage of the opportunity to be there. Use it as a time to research the show for next year, or to just make some new connections in your industry. Save time, money and stress!

Start by setting goals, just like you would if you were exhibiting. What do you want to accomplish? Do you want to observe the show itself, study your competition, or network with attendees? You can achieve all of these things.

Register early, so you will receive pre-show promotions. See how much you receive from exhibitors and how much from show management. Evaluate the registration process and logistics of the show itself.

Ask your suppliers, clients and prospects if they will be attending the show. Schedule appointments with them (off the show floor), or arrange to meet them for lunch or dinner. Scan your contact files for people who live in the show's host city. These people may also be available to meet with you while you're in town.

Before you arrive, study the show directory or Web site and plan an agenda for each day. Decide on which educational sessions you will attend. Then walk the show. Scope out your competition. How big are their booths? Are they drawing a crowd? Study the quality and quantity of attendees. Do they meet your expectations?

Be sure to cover the entire show floor at least twice. That way, you can get a feel for the entire show, but still go back to gather details. A word of caution: Don't ever solicit on the show floor! You didn't buy a booth, so you shouldn't be selling at the show. In fact, at most shows, if you get caught soliciting, you will be thrown out!

Afterwards, record your observations and create an idea file of things you've learned for use in planning future shows.

such as that the promotional efforts were bad or the show's floor plan was not attendee-friendly.

A few other things to ask about before you sign: The availability of parking (especially if it's a consumer show), the booth cancellation policy (if there is one), and whether there are opportunities to have a representative from your company on the speaking schedule (a great way to gain exposure).

Did you know?

➻ 83% of <u>qualified attendees</u> have an influence on buying decisions and 38% have the final say. (*Source: Exhibit Surveys Inc., CEIR Report #AC/RR 1130*)
➻ 37% of consumer show attendees make a purchase at a show. (*Source: CEIR Report #AC27B*)
➻ 56% plan to make a purchase within 12 months. (*Source: Exhibit Surveys Inc.*)

Another good research technique is to ask your customers or prospects which shows they attend. (If you hear the same two or three show names popping up over and over, then that's where you need to be.) Find out how long they spend at each show, and whether or not they would recommend it to their colleagues. Ask if they made any purchases as a result of last year's show. Most importantly, find out what product categories they felt were over-saturated and what types of products were missing. Even if it's a great show, if 17 of your competitors are already exhibiting, would you be able to stand out?

If you have questions or concerns about a certain show, check with the Trade Show Exhibitors Association (TSEA) or the International Association of Exhibition Managers (IAEM). These two organizations are the heart of the trade show industry and can

> Don't blow your entire exhibiting budget on one show! It's better to do three or four smaller shows in different areas, perhaps with a slightly larger booth than you could afford at one (more expensive) major show. Be a big fish in a small pond!

give you an objective look at a specific show. (See listings in the Resource section.)

If a show is sponsored by a particular magazine, take a look at the publication's existing demographics. If you're already advertising in that publication, what kind of response have you had? If you've never advertised with them, check with some who have. Find out if they also exhibit at the show and what kind of results they've seen.

If the show's sponsor is an association, are you a member? What is the show's reputation in its industry? If you're not a member, find out how much more it will cost you to exhibit (many shows have discounted booth fees for members). Perhaps you will want to go ahead and join the organization to save some money (often there are package deals for joining and exhibiting), as well as to gain access to the membership mailing list.

Once you've done your homework, go back to show management and ask what kind of promotions they do. What publications do they advertise in? (You might even want to make some suggestions.) Do they accept pre-registrations? If so, do they make that list available to you for pre-show mailings? What tools do they make available for exhibitors to use in promotions? (More on this in Chapter 8: Creating Curb Appeal.)

The current trend in the exhibit industry is for more highly targeted shows, geared to specific niche markets. For example, instead of a general computer show, there is one targeted to Web site designers. While the audience may be smaller, the AIF is much higher. This is what's known as a vertical show.

> "Most people don't recognize opportunity because it comes disguised as hard work."
>
> - Anonymous

Some other factors to consider before booking your booth space:

• Dates (If it falls too close to another show, it might be more than you can handle.)

• Timing (The best spaces fill up quickly, and you don't want to miss the early bird discount rates!)

• Pay a visit (If you're planning long-range, attend the show this year and see for yourself how it fits with your company image and goals, before deciding to exhibit next year.)

Once you've researched all the shows of interest to your company, rank them by the most relevant and the most reasonable. Then make your selections!

 ## Vocabulary

Audit: verification of attendance figures by an agency independent of show management

Exhibitor Prospectus: promotional materials used to encourage a prospective exhibitor to participate in the show

Exhibitor Appointed Contractor (EAC): company selected by an individual exhibitor to provide specific show services; must be approved by show management

General Service Contractor (GSC): company designated by show management to provide all labor and services for exhibitors at the show

Qualified attendees: people who have a legitimate reason to be at the show

Resources

ABC Expomark
847-879-8272
www.abcexpomark.com

International Association for Exhibition Management (IAEM)
972-458-8002
www.iaem.org

Trade Show Exhibitors Association (TSEA)
312-842-8732
www.tsea.org

Trade Show Directory Listings:

Tradeshow Week Data Book
323-965-5300
www.tradeshowweek.com

TSNN (online directory)
www.tsnn.com

"When we
mean to build,
We first survey
the plot,
then draw
the model."

– Shakespeare
(from Henry IV)

Draw a Blueprint

Trade Show Success Formula

- 40% Pre-show (Planning)
- 20% At show (Behavior & technique)
- 40% Post-show (Follow-up & ROI)

Just like building a house starts with a blueprint, trade show exhibiting must start with a plan! Once you've determined your goals and decided which shows you want to participate in, you have to put together a detailed blueprint for everyone involved to follow.

Have a brainstorming session with people from various departments involved in the exhibiting process (accounting, marketing, sales, public relations, technical, product design, etc.). If you let everyone have a say in the planning, you're much more likely to get their support in all stages of the project. Make sure you communicate your company's exhibiting objectives to each person involved, so they're all working toward the same goal. Otherwise, some may form their own ideas as to why you're exhibiting.

Exhibitor's Timeline

Don't manage by committee! Assign one person to be in charge of the timeline and coordinate all aspects of planning. Then delegate the various responsibilities. Keep notes on each stage of the process to help make things run more smoothly for future shows.

> The bigger your exhibit, the more planning that needs to go into it, just like a skyscraper requires a deeper foundation than a three-story building.

Exhibitor's Timeline

10 - 12 Months Before Show
- Research & select shows (Chapter 2)
- Begin planning/set goals (Chapter 1)
- Define target audience (Chapter 1)
- Establish budget
- Reserve booth space
- Book hotel/airline
- Plan booth theme (Chapter 4)

6 - 10 Months Before Show
- Evaluate current display (reuse, revamp or start over?)
- Study show rules and regulations (before constructing booth)
- Design booth layout (Chapter 5)
- Select staffers (Chapter 6 and 7)
- Plan publicity and promotions (Chapter 8, 9 and 10)
- Order signage
- Plan hospitality events (Chapter 14)

3 - 6 Months Before Show
- Determine product to be displayed
- Arrange for shipping
- Finalize display and learn how to assemble it (even if it will actually be done by union labor)
- Order supplies and equipment needed (audio/visual, floral, computer, furniture, etc.)
- Study Exhibitor Manual – order show services now to save more (carpet, electrical, plumbing, booth cleaning, phone, security, etc.)
- Develop and compile targeted mailing list
- Design pre-show mailers and booth literature (Chapter 8)
- Register all booth personnel

2 - 3 Months Before Show
- Print pre-show mailers
- Design press kits (Chapter 10)
- Send press releases (you may need to do this earlier, depending on publication schedules) (Chapter 10)
- Order premiums/giveaways (Chapter 8 and 9)
- Design <u>lead cards</u> (Chapter 11)
- Begin pre-show marketing/mailings
- Train booth staff (Chapter 6 and 7)
- Confirm all travel reservations and make restaurant reservations for staff or hospitality events
- Appoint someone to oversee installation & dismantling (I&D)

One Month Before Show
- Verify show services
- Assemble display in-house and make last-minute adjustments
- Confirm product samples/literature
- Continue pre-show promotions (Chapter 8)
- Finalize booth staff schedule
- Ship display and materials (exhibit display and graphics, product displays, literature and giveaways)
- Practice in-booth demonstrations (Know how to work all equipment!)

Three Weeks Before Show
- Mail final pre-show promotions
- Send last-minute reminders to media (Chapter 10)

One Week Before Show
- Organize items to take to the show (tool kit, copies of all contracts, contact names and numbers for show management and services, exhibit emergency kit) (See page 33.)

- Finalize follow-up plan (Chapter 11)
- Do role-playing with staff (engaging, overcoming objections, etc.) (Chapter 7)
- Confirm all shipments

Set-Up Day
- Know your move-in schedule!
- Hold a staff briefing to review goals and techniques
- Supervise setup of booth (have photos of the finished booth for reference)

During the Show
- Hold daily team meetings to keep staff informed and to track progress (Chapter 6)
- Keep booth neat and clean
- Book space for next year

After the Show
- Supervise booth dismantling and move-out
- Have a team meeting and evaluate show results (Chapter 12)
- Distribute leads; begin follow-up ASAP! (Chapter 11)
- Send customized follow-up packets (Chapter 11)
- Send thank-you notes to staff
- Begin planning next year's show (Chapter 1)

Shipping Tips

All the best planning in the world won't save you if your booth isn't where you want it, on time and intact. To help make sure that happens, David Mihalik of ELITeXPO, a trade show shipping company, offers the following tips.

1.   Whenever possible, use new cartons or crates.
Don't keep reusing the same cartons that have made numerous trips to shows. New cartons not only offer better protection for your display, but also will keep any claims for damage from being denied due to poor packaging.

2. Pack for easy unloading and setup.
Use the "last in, first out" method: pack your carpet and pad last, along with your cables and tools so they will be the first thing out when it comes time for setup. Also be sure to number your crates and keep a packing list with you, so you know what's in each crate.

3. Make sure contents are secure, both inside and out.
There should be no audible movement inside the cartons if they are shaken. Be sure to add cushioning materials, but don't use foam peanuts (they're messy and don't work well). If you use shrink-wrap, use dark instead of clear to conceal the contents. Secure the outside with strong, clear packaging tape. Placing large, legible address labels directly on the seam, both top and bottom, provides a sure-fire way to determine if your cartons have been opened for any reason.

4. Make sure your address labels are correct.
Sending a carton addressed to the convention center itself, with no further info, will result in a lost or refused delivery. Be sure to include your company name, the show name, booth number,

> "Wisdom is knowing what to do next, skill is knowing how to do it, and success is doing it."
>
> - Anonymous

and the name and address of the delivery location (either advance receiving or the show site), contact name, and phone number. (Check with your shipper for labels to use.) And always remove old labels after the show to avoid confusion the next time you ship.

5. Save time at teardown by applying outbound labels to empty cartons during setup. Then be sure to label the cartons "empty" for

---

 Suggested Budget Guidelines

These are basic guidelines. Each exhibitor's situation is different.

Booth space	25%
Exhibit Design/Graphics	18%
(prorated over life of exhibit; including refurbishment and modifications)	
Show Services	14%
(drayage, I&D, electrical, cleaning, etc.)	
Travel/Lodging	13%
(includes client entertainment)	
Shipping	9%
Promotions	10%
(pre-show and in-booth; press kits, literature, giveaways, prizes, sponsorships and ads)	
Lead Management and ROI Measurement	5%
Personnel/Staffing	5%
(training, uniforms, registrations)	
Other expenses	1%

Analyze where the money is going, then decide in which categories to adjust spending. Some areas where you can usually cut costs include: exhibit design, shipping, show services, promotions, printing, and staffing. (For money-saving tips on each of these, see the sidebar on page 30.)

storage by the GSC during the show. Anything you want returned to your booth at the end of the show needs this label, including pallets, so that the GSC knows which items are to be stored instead of thrown away.

6. Make sure that your carrier has several emergency numbers they can use to contact you in the event of a delay, or any other situation that needs your attention. These numbers should include your voice mail, e-mail, pager, cell phone, home or other after-hours number, as well as numbers for alternate contacts. Be sure to get your carrier's emergency numbers, too.

 Exhibit Fix-Its

- ☛ Clean your graphics and laminate surfaces periodically (using appropriate cleaners)
- ☛ Touch up chips and scratches on display
- ☛ Camouflage major holes
- ☛ Use a lint brush on fabric surfaces
- ☛ Have extra nuts & bolts on hand at setup
- ☛ Allow 25% of the display's initial cost for annual <u>refurbishment</u>

---

7. Choose a carrier whose primary function is the shipping of trade show materials.
Most shows have a surcharge or higher <u>drayage</u> rate for small packages delivered by UPS, FedEx or other such methods. (Instead, simply carry any last-minute items with you to the show.) Trade show carriers are experts in shipping to shows and can handle all of the "freight management" details that you would have to pay other vendors to manage for you.

8. Don't ever try to argue with labor unions on the floor.
You may win the battle, but plan on losing the war. Be nice to the workers who are returning your empty cartons or crates, but don't reward them until AFTER you've received your property. (Keep in mind that some show halls prohibit giving and accepting gratuities. Always check the local rules first.) If you really want to reward

them, consider providing bottled water or snacks instead of simply giving tips.

9. Create a unique marking or design on your cartons or crates.

One idea is to paint the corners of all your crates

Cutting Costs Without Sacrificing Anything

•• Plan ahead! Reserve booth space and show services early to take advantage of discounts, and avoid overtime rates at the facility.

•• Scale back the number of staff to those who absolutely must attend, or use temporary staff in the host city for basic duties like greeting attendees or scanning badges.

•• Use e-mail and Web promotions to save on postage.

•• Consolidate shipping. Charges are usually rounded to the next hundred pounds or CWT (one hundred weight). Bundle smaller things together to make one larger shipment. Also, be sure to ship far enough in advance to avoid paying any "rush" charges.

•• If you have a fairly full show schedule, simply ship from one show to the next instead of back to the home office each time. (Or, if you have a branch office in or near the show city, ship to them instead of to the show warehouse.)

•• If you plan to give out lots of literature or giveaways (which will eliminate boxes to be return shipped) and have a multi-year partnership with the GSC, ask about a one-way adjustment on your drayage charges.

•• Take your own trash can, extension cords and power strips with you, instead of renting them at the show.

•• Use one theme for all your exhibits in a year, then order promotional materials and giveaways in bulk (this also helps save money on exhibit design/graphics and staff uniforms).

•• Use existing artwork on your booth graphics and promotions. Not only will it save money, but it also reinforces your company message.

a certain color, perhaps your corporate color. Even better, paint the entire crate. This not only helps you locate your crates on the show floor, but also helps your carrier locate your materials in case they lose track of them.

10. ALWAYS complete a <u>Bill of Lading</u> from the General Service Contractor at the show site. The purpose of this document is to get a receipt that the GSC has control of your freight and instructions on what to do with it. You should keep accurate records of how many crates you

 Trimming Travel Costs

➡ Plan for travel on Tuesday, Wednesday or Saturday to get the best deals.

➡ Look on the Web to check airfares, but if you need more than simple round-trip air, consult a travel agent who can explore possibilities you might never find on your own (such as an air/hotel package that is less than the cost of airfare alone). By using a travel agent, you'll also have an advocate if some thing goes wrong.

➡ Choose alternate airports (Midway vs. O'Hare, Burbank vs. Los Angeles International) to save both time and money.

➡ Sign up for a corporate credit card through your preferred air line to accumulate mileage, then use it for all trip-related expenses. Many of these cards also have special partnerships with certain hotel chains or car rental agencies.

➡ Have staffers room together.

➡ Join a hotel "frequent traveler" program.

➡ Look for hotels that provide a free breakfast.

➡ Give staffers corporate phone cards (with limited usage of the cards) to save on hotel phone charges.

(Tips courtesy of Kathy Sudeikis from All About Travel)

will be shipping, as well as their actual weight. Keep in mind the GSC is not responsible for any losses that occur until the freight reaches your carrier's truck. This means you need to take responsibility to watch the cartons until they are loaded. Be sure to designate your carrier, or else the GSC will use the show's carrier, meaning your shipment will arrive "collect" and you must pay up before receiving your materials.

Resources

ELITeXPO
800-543-5484
www.elitexpo.com

Vocabulary

Bill of Lading: document serving as contract between a shipper and a transportation company that outlines how and where freight will be moved

Drayage: transporting your materials from the loading dock to the booth, storing crates during the show, and getting it all back to the dock after the show

I&D: installation and dismantling (set-up and tear down) of the booth; provided by an appointed contractor

Lead cards: forms used to collect demographic and qualifying data on attendees who visit the booth

Overtime rates: higher rates paid to show labor for setup, drayage, etc. that fall outside the usual Monday-to-Friday daytime hours; some locations charge double time on Sunday and holidays

Refurbishment: repairing damages and refinishing display surfaces and graphics to extend the exhibit's lifespan

Trade Show Tool Kit Contents

Office Supplies

❑ Pens/pencils
❑ Staplers/staples/remover
❑ Scissors
❑ Paper clips
❑ Tape (transparent & packing)

❑ Post-It Notes
❑ Calculator
❑ Ruler/tape measure
❑ Clipboards
❑ Rubber bands

Business Tools

❑ Lead cards (Ch. 11)
❑ Order forms/contracts
❑ Price lists
❑ Press releases/press kits (Ch. 10)
❑ Company letterhead/envelopes
❑ Giveaways/prizes/promotions (Ch. 9)
❑ Staff list & booth schedule (with contact numbers)
❑ Return labels for shipping back display & supplies

❑ Exhibitor kit/forms
❑ Copies of advance orders
❑ Literature/catalogs
❑ Appointment book
❑ Business cards
❑ Booth staffing manual

Tools

❑ Set-up tools
❑ Utility knife
❑ Hand vac
❑ Carpet tape
❑ Touch-up paint
❑ Extension cords/3-way adapters
❑ Disposable camera (to take booth photos)

❑ Printer cartridges/cables
❑ Software
❑ Flashlight
❑ Cleaning supplies
❑ Level
❑ Velcro fabric fasteners

Personal/Travel Supplies

❑ Airline tickets
❑ Hotel & car rental info
❑ First-Aid kit
❑ Sewing kit with safety pins
❑ Lemon drops (for a tired voice)
❑ Show badges
❑ Cushioned shoe inserts/extra shoes
❑ "S" hooks (good for hanging things on pipe & drape)

❑ Wet wipes/hand sanitizer
❑ Bottled water
❑ Pre-paid phone card
❑ Small mirror
❑ Hand lotion
❑ Pain relievers
❑ Shoe polish

Fictional Case Study: DigiCrayon

Scenario:
A small educational software company who wants to showcase their newest creation: a landscape design program, featuring an online gardening guide

Show:
Local Home & Garden Show, estimated 20,000 attendees over three days (28 hours); a horizontal consumer show

Exhibit:
10' x 10' booth

Goals:
Out of those who stop at the booth:
- Sell 250 software packages ($49.95 retail at a show special of $35; $8,750 total sales)
- Gather mailing list of 500 names
- Gain local media coverage (at least 2 stories)

Breakdown:
18 leads and 9 sales per hour

Budget:
$1,000	Space rental
$ 750	Booth design
$ 800	Show services
$ 750	Promotions
$ 400	Staffing
$ 300	Misc. expenses
$4,000	

(Since DigiCrayon is a local company, they won't have any travel or shipping expenses, so they can spend more in other areas.)

Fictional Case Study: Purple Carrot Press

Scenario:

A children's book publisher wants to showcase their new line of collateral materials (stuffed toys, games, puzzles); two main characters to feature: Sunny the Frog and Alyssa

Show:

Regional book and toy retailers' show with an estimated 7,000 attendees over two days (14 hours); a vertical trade show

Exhibit:

20' x 30' island booth

Goals:

Out of those who stop at the booth:
- Gain 550 leads (stores to possibly carry products)
- Sign up 100 new retailers within 30 days of show
- Gain media coverage (at least one TV and one print)

Breakdown:

40 leads per hour

Budget:

$10,000	Space rental
$ 7,500	Booth design & new graphics
$8,000	Show services
$5,000	Shipping
$6,500	Travel & lodging (10 staffers)
$8,000	Promotions
$2,500	Staffing
$2,500	Misc. expenses
$50,000	

(Purple Carrot Press has chosen to adjust their budget slightly to allow for more promotions. You'll find find out why later!)

"Strong themes create multiple places within a place ... The more sensory an experience, the more memorable it will be."

– From **The Experience Economy,** by Joseph Pine & James Gilmore

Starting to Build

When you build a house, you wouldn't start by simply stacking up bricks on the ground to form the walls, would you?

Of course not! Neither should you start your exhibit plan by just throwing objects together to create a display. You must first determine how all the elements of your exhibiting plan will tie together to make one unified marketing message. The booth display, promotions, in-booth attractions, and even post-show follow-up should all stem from one comprehensive, thought-provoking blueprint, which brings us to ...

The Importance of a Good Foundation

When you start constructing your exhibit plan, you have to begin by defining your basic message or theme. Often this is an extension of your overall marketing campaign – just think of your booth as a three-dimensional ad!

Don't assume that all you need is an impressive booth display to guarantee success. It's only half of the building process. To be truly successful, you need to tie together both the design and content of your booth to effectively convey your message.

Building a Successful Exhibit

Exterior (Design)	**Interior (Content)**
• Space Rental	• Pre-Show Promos
• Booth Construction	• Staffers
• Graphics	• Literature
• Shipping/Logistics/I&D	• Giveaways
• Show Services	• Follow-up

Most exhibitors spend more time & money in this column; up to 90% of total budget

Should be real focus – provides biggest return; often only 10% of budget

(Source: CEIR Report #SM22)

A theme helps to give your exhibit focus and make your message more memorable for attendees. To be most effective, it should be incorporated into all elements of your exhibit marketing, not just the display itself. Don't just look for a gimmick – your theme needs to trigger an emotional response.

 # Exhibit Memorability Statistics

Exhibit Surveys Inc., which analyzes shows from various industries, has found that certain factors play a major role in how likely attendees are to remember an exhibit several weeks after the show. This includes being able to recall the company name and basic information about its products. The longer an attendee remembers a particular exhibit, the more likely he or she is to purchase from that company when a need arises. Percentages in this list are based on how many people listed each factor as a reason they remember an exhibit.

Product Interest	64%
Well-known Company	51%
Product Demonstration	43%
Stage/Theater Presentation	26%
Exhibit Color or Design	19%
Personnel	18%
Giveaways	15%
Literature	13%

A few words of caution:
- The larger the exhibit, the higher the memorability; however, even a small booth in the back corner can make a big impact with a well-planned exhibit.
- Don't be mislead by the fact that booth staff ranks low on the list. People are key to results! If your staff is poorly trained, they won't help with exhibit memorability at all, and may even negatively influence visitors.
- Demonstrations are even more memorable when they require the audience to interact. (More on this in Chapter 9: Impressing the Neighbors.)

Your theme doesn't have to be expensive in order to compete with the big guys. In fact, some very clever and memorable exhibits have been done with very small budgets. Besides, if you don't break the bank on your exhibit, it will be that much easier to change your theme periodically.

• The Charlotte (N.C.) Convention & Visitors Bureau wanted to make a creative splash at the annual meeting for the American Society of

---

 Designing a Theme Without Breaking the Bank

When engineering construction firm Sverdrup Civil Inc. decided to use a football theme to reinforce the idea that their consulting engineers "coach customers," Jeanne Harwin, assistant director of marketing, didn't have a huge budget to work with. Using a stock photo of a giant crowd for the backdrop, PVC pipe goal posts, and artificial grass, Harwin was able to create the illusion of being on the field. With staff dressed like coaches (with whistles and clipboards), and a football toss competition for attendees, the theme was complete. And Harwin was able to pull this off in a 10' x 20' space!

To develop a winning theme on a bare bones budget, Harwin offers the following tips:

• Look at your audience and appeal to their interests
• Keep asking "what if" to discover low-cost alternative props that bring the theme to life
• Buy items locally at garden shops, sporting goods stores, or novelty shops
• Use event planners to rent props in the show city
• Reuse your graphics (Sverdrup has also used the crowd graphic for a racing theme and a baseball theme)
• Check out the local theater industry for costumes and props

> Don't do a theme just to be cute! When used as part of your overall marketing plan, a theme can really reinforce brand. It also helps to distinguish you from all the other exhibits.

Association Executives (ASAE), so they designed an interactive booth display. Pre-show mailers included a small paintbrush, with the message, "Picasso painted until he was 90, but you don't have to wait that long." When they arrived at the show, attendees were allowed to paint on a large, two-sided display wall standing in the center of the booth. The Charlotte CVB provided bright-colored paint, various rollers and brushes, and smocks for their guests. Even those who chose not to paint gathered to watch the artists at work. After each wall had been covered with art, a nearly invisible white mask was carefully removed to reveal the Charlotte skyline in vivid color! The final mural was featured on a follow-up postcard sent to attendees after the show.

• The DoubleTree Hotel put a bed in their booth and staffers dressed in pajamas and fuzzy slippers at a Meeting Professionals International show. They offered visitors samples of their legendary chocolate chip cookies in little bags with a tag that said, "Have Sweet Dreams at the DoubleTree." The staffers in pajamas were the talk of the show!

• At that same MPI show, the Overland Park (Kan.) Convention & Visitors Bureau wanted to feature the construction of their new Convention Center. The booth was decorated with yellow construction tape and hard hats and featured an architect's 3-D model of the new center. Visitors were offered yellow hard hat key chains imprinted with the CVB's name. At the reception they sponsored, attendees were served ice cream in yellow hard hat cups.

Just in case you're thinking, "OK, but they are really creative people. I could never come up with something like that," here are some tips to get you started.

First of all, gather your company brochures, product descriptions, catalogs, and other sales literature. Then interview clients to find out what they like best about your product or company (you may uncover some great testimonials this way). Next, study your current ad campaign and web site for recurring messages and possible themes. Once you have all this information, decide on the main message you want to convey. Simplify! Remember to use everyday language, not industry jargon.

How do you determine your message? Start by answering the following questions about your company:

- Who are you?
- What do you do?
- Who are your current clients?
- What do you want people to think of when they think of you?
- What "picture" do you create?
- What is your corporate personality?
- Do customers really know what you do? Or do they have "tunnel vision"?

Brainstorm with your staff. Boil your message down to between three and five sentences, then pick out the one major concept. Look for a metaphor you can build your message around that will reinforce your main concept. For example, if you want to emphasize that you provide more reliable or dependable service, use the story of the tortoise and the hare, where "Steady wins the race." If you're focusing on all the services you can provide, use the theme of a restaurant with a "menu of services."

Keys to a Winning Theme

- Make it current – tie in with current trends or events
- Avoid cliche or overused themes
- Follow your corporate personality (consistency)
- Play off the show's theme or location
- KISS ("Keep it smart and simple")
- Get your whole team involved in the planning process
- Hit an emotional nerve; play on attendees' memories of childhood or a great place

Suppose your main message is to show that, although you are the little guy (or new kid on the industry block), your product can outshine the big guys. You could go several different ways with your theme:

Road Race – "Miles Ahead of the Competition"
Detective/Secret Agent – "Discover the Secrets of the XYZ Machine"
Pirate – "Unlock the Hidden Treasures of the XYZ Machine"
Safari – "Explore a New Way to _____"
Sports – "Winning with the XYZ Machine" (could also play up underdog theme)
Medical – "We Diagnose Your Problem and Prescribe the Solution"

Once you have decided on your core message, you can begin to put all the elements together. Keep it consistent! Your theme should be conveyed throughout your pre-show mailers, booth display, giveaways, follow-up materials, and more. You're essentially telling a story, so make sure everything follows one story line, working together to help attendees remember your core message.

Still at a loss for a great theme? Ideas can come from anywhere – TV, movies, magazines, children's stories, travel locations – the possibilities are endless! The basic list on the next page can help get you started brainstorming. (One word of caution: if you decide to go with a movie or television show as a theme, be sure to check first that you won't be in violation of any copyright or trademark infringements!)

Some examples of a theme in action:

• Wood Associates (a promotional products company) played off a show's location in Washington D.C. during an election year by

> In a brainstorming session, nothing is off-limits. Write everything down without criticizing anyone. Review all the ideas and then choose the top ones.

using the theme "Wood Associates Wants You." Their pre-show mailer was a button featuring Uncle Sam and their tag line. Attendees wearing the button received gifts including teddy bears dressed in red or blue t-shirts and the classic white "campaign" hat with a red, white and blue ribbon on it. Instead of lead cards, they used "ballots" to collect information.

• Transformit, a company that creates tension fabric structures, wanted to feature their new line of "Organics" designs at The Special Event, a show for the special events industry. Since the signature piece of the new line was the "Morning Glory" (which actually "blooms" with computer animation), they created the theme "Seeds of Imagination," according to Marc Posnock, Transformit's Director of Marketing. Using artwork that resembled old-fashioned seed packets, pre-show postcards were sent to invite attendees to the "Garden of Earthly Delights." The exhibit looked like a gigantic

> **Define what impression you want visitors to leave your booth with, and then design cues that will create that impression.**

Possible Theme Ideas

Construction Site	Road Race
Castle/Fairy Tale Kingdom/Medieval	Dinosaurs
High Seas/Deep Sea	Rainforest
Detective/Secret Agent	Beach
Picasso/Monet/Other Artists	Hollywood
Cheerleading/Sports	Outer Space
Kitchen/Chefs/Diner/Coffee House	Wild West
Safari/Zoo/Outback	Medical
Old South	Hawaii/Luau
New Orleans/Mardi Gras	Egyptian
New York/Broadway	Greek/Roman
70s/50s/other time period	Wizard of Oz

Standing Out

To stand out on the show floor, sometimes it's as simple as black & white!

When everyone else is using bright colors, you could create a design that "pops" with black and white and maybe a bit of red for accent. (Think of the 50's diner look.)

garden in full bloom. Staffers gave away t-shirts with the same seed packet graphic on the front. Post-show mailings included an actual packet of Morning Glory seeds. (Posnock reports that the campaign was used at three shows, won several awards and generated 15 percent more leads than the previous year.)

• The Newport (R.I.) and Providence/Warwick CVBs wanted to make a lasting impression at a show for meeting planners, so they partnered with hometown toy maker Hasbro to develop a fun and memorable theme. Using items donated by Hasbro, the CVB mailed out Mr. Potato Head toys, one piece at a time. Each piece was accompanied by a clue about the sender. While in the booth, visitors had the opportunity to play Hasbro games and get their photo taken with a costumed Mr. Potato Head character (this also provided time for the staff to talk with those standing in line). The CVBs gathered double the usual number of leads collected that year, according to Martha Sheridan, Vice President of Sales for the Newport CVB. The partnership with Hasbro was the result of some creative brainstorming, and provided a win-win for both the CVB and the toy company. The partnership has continued, Sheridan reports, with exhibits themed around the Operation game ("We've got a funny bone to pick with you") and "Twister Rhode Island Style" (with the "circles" sponsored by various Rhode Island hotels and services).

• Bankers Advertising, another promotional products company, created a "Recipe for Success." Pre-show mailers included a potholder imprinted with the booth number and the message, "Mention this potholder and receive a free gift." Laura Wissel, trade show coordinator for Bankers, says they were overwhelmed with the response and amazed at how many people actually brought their potholder to the booth! At the show, the theme continued with giveaways of snack foods and stress balls shaped like hamburgers and various vegetables. Even their follow-up mailers were printed on recipe cards.

Once your foundation of an exhibiting plan and basic marketing message are in place, only then can you begin to build on it.

Fictional Case Study: DigiCrayon

Scenario:

A small educational software company who wants to showcase their newest creation: a landscape design program, featuring an online gardening guide

Show:

Local Home & Garden Show, estimated 20,000 attendees over three days (28 hours); a horizontal consumer show

Exhibit:

10' x 10' booth

Goals:

Out of those who stop at the booth:
- Sell 250 software packages ($49.95 retail at a show special of $35; $8,750 total sales)
- Gather mailing list of 500 names
- Gain local media coverage (at least 2 stories)

Breakdown:

18 leads and 9 sales per hour

Budget:

$1,000	Space rental
$ 750	Booth design
$ 800	Show services
$ 750	Promotions
$ 400	Staffing
$ 300	Misc. expenses
$4,000	

Theme:

"Where Technology Blooms"

Fictional Case Study: Purple Carrot Press

Scenario:

A children's book publisher wants to showcase their new line of collateral materials (stuffed toys, games, puzzles); two main characters to feature: Sunny the Frog and Alyssa

Show:

Regional book and toy retailers' show with an estimated 7,000 attendees over two days (14 hours); a vertical trade show

Exhibit:

20' x 30' island booth

Goals:

Out of those who stop at the booth:
- Gain 550 leads (stores to possibly carry products)
- Sign up 100 new retailers within 30 days of show
- Gain media coverage (at least one TV and one print)

Breakdown:

40 leads per hour

Budget:

$10,000	Space rental
$ 7,500	Booth design & new graphics
$8,000	Show services
$5,000	Shipping
$6,500	Travel & lodging (10 staffers)
$8,000	Promotions
$2,500	Staffing
$2,500	Misc. expenses
$50,000	

Theme:

"More than Just a Story"

Rise above the
confusion! If
you create
a unique
experience,
people are
certain to
remember
your booth.

Creating the Framework

For the duration of the show, your booth is your storefront, so design it accordingly. You must create a unique identity in a sea of other exhibits.

Think billboard! Just like on the highway, you only have five to seven seconds to capture your audience's attention and convey your main message. Your booth shouldn't look like a catalog of everything you have to offer. People are basically "cruising" the aisles. If you've got too much going on in the booth, people will choose to move on. Keep it understated with your product or service as the main focus.

If you want your booth to last for several years, don't design it to be too trendy!

Elements of Your Exhibit Image:
- Company Identity
- Product Presentation
  (covered in Chapter 9)
- Booth Design
- Booth Staff (covered in Chapter 6)

Booth Design Basics

A well-designed booth should be: Inviting, Entertaining, Educational, and Memorable.

When designing the booth, make what you do and the ways you can help meet the attendees' needs (benefits) the most prominent elements, followed by your company name. Give them a reason to buy from you. Offer "real-world" examples of problems you can solve – be sure to think from the audience's viewpoint. Promote benefits, not features. And never, ever knock your competition!

Use large type in a standard font that can be easily read from the aisle (a recommended 1" tall for every 3 feet away that attendees will be) and keep it to seven words or less (just like a billboard). It also needs to be high enough to be seen over the heads of people in the booth. Use plain language – avoid industry jargon, even if you're exhibiting at an industry show.

Make your graphics large and powerful, not a collage of little images. (Remember: Think billboard, not bulletin board!) Repeat graphics from your marketing materials to create a consistent image. Include props that are both attractive and functional, such as a baker's rack for product displays or literature, unusual picture frames with product photos or satisfied customer quotes, or a three-dimensional company logo.

> **Load all your fonts and logos onto a disk in case you need to redo any panels at the show.**

 Keys to Creating Great Graphics

- ➹ Select dynamic images that make people do a double-take.
- ➹ Use backlit graphics for emphasis.
- ➹ Start planning your graphics far enough in advance to avoid stress and rush charges (at least three months out).
- ➹ When submitting graphics to a designer, be sure to include any special fonts used, specify any Pantone colors, and double-check what image resolution is needed.
- ➹ Viewing distance should equal two times the diagonal measurement of your final graphic (for example, if your graphic measures 10 feet, all wording should be visible from at least 20 feet).

- Marc Muccino and Dave Atkins,
Custom Color Corporation

Tie your entire display together with carpeting in colors that coordinate, or possibly incorporate your logo or a message in the carpet.

Use lighting to reinforce your theme and create a three-dimensional feeling with light and shadows, in addition to showing off products. Light can create mood, drama and alter the existing space to either conceal areas or make them seem more open. One popular technique is to use gobos – theatrical lights with screens that create a "floating" message on the walls or floor of your booth (or even on water). These rotating images can also be designed to change color periodically. According to Jerry Swatek of Upstaging, Inc., a theatrical lighting company, technology has enabled the automation to become more efficient.

"Although lighting is an intimidating area for many exhibitors, it doesn't have to be," Swatek says. "Have an open dialog with your exhibit designer or lighting house, and remember you don't have to figure it all out yourself."

Walk through any given show and you'll see an abundance of pop-up and hardwall modular displays. But the cookie-cutter look of the 1980s and 1990s is changing. One surface gaining popularity is the brushed metal look, particularly for high-tech and fashion

Lighting Effects Defined

Accent lighting: "lighting for emphasis"; places focus on specific products; intensity much brighter than surrounding light; can bring character, texture and dimension to featured items

Architectural lighting: used to sculpt and define the exhibit structure, enhancing the personality of booth; can use white or colored light or projected patterns

Performance lighting: spotlights live performers in the booth or a new product unveiling

Special effect lighting: attention-getters; often moving light with color changes or special effects; can project custom images or logos

Source: Jerry Swatek, Upstaging Inc.

companies. A more traditional, yet unique option is faux granite. But with either of these surfaces, you need to incorporate other elements that help to soften the look and make it more inviting.

It's a good idea to make a swatch chart of the various materials and colors you plan to use, just like an interior designer would.

A growing trend in display design is the use of fabric structures. Cindy Thompson is a sculptor turned display designer who uses fabric fashioned into "playful shapes" to convert a booth into an environment. Her company, Transformit, specializes in versatile, freestanding structures that "tap into people's emotions." When combined with theatrical lighting, the designs can be used to create a mood, or a variety of moods, simply by changing the color of the lights. "We have the concept of selling dreams and experiences," says Marc Posnock, Director of Marketing for Transformit. In addition to being warm and inviting, fabric can also create a coziness by separating a large booth into private spaces.

Should You Rent or Buy?

Before you buy a new display, consider how long you plan to use it. Then calculate your cost per show. Factor in some of the "hidden costs" of owning an exhibit, which include: I&D expenses (how much labor is required to set it up), shipping (weight and bulk), storage, and costs for cleaning and refurbishing. These can total 20 percent or more of the original exhibit cost ... per year!

(Note: For the purpose of the following example, the exhibitors chose to have a very creative display that changes frequently. A typical exhibit display should last about three to five years, and the pop-up display frame will last even longer, according to exhibit design experts.)

Example 1:

$ 10,000 booth design cost
+ $ 8,000 related expenses
$ 18,000 total booth cost
÷ _____ 2 years
$ 9,000 cost per year
÷ _____ 10 shows per year
$ 900 cost per show

Example 2:

$ 10,000 booth design cost
+ $ 5,000 related expenses
$ 15,000 total booth cost
÷ _____ 2 years
$ 7,500 cost per year
÷ _____ 2 shows per year
$ 3,750 cost per show

> Having a sign in your booth doesn't mean the black and white cardboard one hung by the show's decorator. That's only to help you find your booth space!

The first exhibitor will probably feel that their display is well worth the money. However, the second exhibitor may not be able to justify the high expense, yet still wants to have that image. One solution may be to rent the booth.

More companies are renting exhibits than ever before, because they desire the flexibility to change their display often, according to Tim Roberts of Catalyst Exhibits. Rentals range from pop-up portables to totally custom looks. "People come to shows to see what's new," Roberts says. "By renting, the exhibit can be redesigned to maximize your message for each show. If attendees see the same exhibit year after year, they may think the company is going nowhere. Instead, you need to be fresh and new."

You should anticipate rental costs to run any-where from 25 to 33 percent of the cost of a new exhibit, Roberts says. So by renting, the second exhibitor's costs could be reduced to about $2,500 per show (25 percent of the initial cost of the booth), and they wouldn't be worried about storing or repairing their exhibit.

How do you know whether to rent or buy your booth? If you have a one-time scheduling conflict or need a special booth size for a certain show, renting is a good alternative. Also, if you want to test out a new design or your company is going through an "image transition," you should opt to rent, instead of buying a booth you may not use again. But if you do numerous shows each year that don't conflict with each other, or

Renting vs. Buying an Exhibit

	Pros	Cons
Renting	Not responsible for storage or refurbishment Costs can be expensed out, instead of depreciated Allows for one-time use of display Smaller investment allows for larger budget on promotions, hospitality events, or other exhibit aspects	May be restricted in choices by available rental displays May be hidden penalties if you back out of a show (check your contract)
Buying	Entire exhibit can be customized to your specification Provides a consistent booth design More cost-effective if exhibiting at numerous shows	No flexibility for unusual booth configurations

if you find yourself renting more than three or four times a year, it would be to your advantage to go ahead and buy a new display.

Beyond the Basics

Work with your exhibit designer to ensure that your finished booth will meet your needs. Design a display that can be flexible to suit various booth configurations. Consider designing the booth with a raised platform if you will be doing product presentations (but make sure it is well

How to Help an Exhibit Designer Help You

- Request to see samples of similar projects done for other clients; ask how these exhibits helped achieve the exhibitors' goals
- Communicate your goals and who your target audience is, as well as your corporate personality and branding
- Bring your collateral materials (brochures, ads, etc.) to the initial meeting to paint a cohesive picture of what you want to communicate
- Ask how long the display will take to set up and tear down (also how many people and tools it will take)
- Let them know if your design will need to be reconfigured for a variety of booth sizes; find out how many cases it will take and if the cases will also need to be "reconfigured"
- Tell them what you will be exhibiting and how many "stations" you need to include (for presentations, product demonstrations, conference areas, etc.)
- Draw up a rough sketch of the look you want (but stay flexible – your designer may have a much better idea)
- Be prepared – the more organized you are, the more you can save in production and overtime costs (Don't change all your plans mid-stream!)

- Tips courtesy of
Brian Bailey, Exhibit Consultant
and Harvey Hacker, Display Designs

Booth Design Costs

•◆ The average booth design cost is $1,230 per linear foot (for inline displays) or $130 per square foot (for island displays).

•◆ Approximately 6% of the display's costs is for graphics.

(Source: Exhibit Designers & Producers Association 2000 Exhibit House Survey)

marked to avoid accidents). A raised area in the booth can also help to discourage the casual looker. Other techniques to use to lower the volume of "tire-kickers" include: using your graphics to prequalify prospects (with words and images that appeal to your target market), keeping giveaways hidden so people have to ask for them, and positioning demonstrations within the booth so they must enter to watch (this also prevents you from blocking the aisles).

Keep in mind the rules and regulations for your specific shows, including height restrictions, and electrical and fire codes (use only Underwriters Laboratories, or UL-approved lighting). Also keep in mind the Americans with Disabilities Act (ADA) restrictions – you want all attendees to be able to access your booth. Don't wait until your booth is all ready to go and then discover that show management won't allow it because it's not in compliance.

Use your booth to illustrate your location and create an environment. If your company is based in New York City, create a "Central Park" setting or a three-dimensional backdrop of the New York skyline. If you're from Los Angeles, include palm trees and the famous Hollywood sign. Make the visitor feel like they are really visiting your business. For example, one cruise line made their booth a replica of one of their ship's cabins, complete with a porthole!

Plan to involve multiple senses in your booth. Ideally, you should appeal to all five!

Sight = visuals, graphics, props
Sound = music, live presentations, video
Smell = scent machine, aromatherapy,
    samples of fragrance products
Touch = hands-on demos, sampling,
    products to pick up
Taste = snacks, food aromas, sample food
    products (for the attendees only, not
    your staff!)

How can you appeal to all the senses? Suppose
your booth has a tropical theme – incorporate
beach sounds, like seagulls and waves. Use props
like a lifeguard chair and beach umbrella; maybe
even some sand. Combine that with the smell

How Can You Stand Out With a 10' x 10' Booth?

• Target your prospects with pre-show promotions
• Have a dynamite staff that is friendly and informative
• Make your display simple, yet dynamic with bold colors
  (feature 1 or 2 products only)
• Use dramatic lighting (consider spotlights on products)
• Provide prompt and thorough follow-up

When Hob Knobs, a manufacturer of hand-painted doorknobs
for cabinets and furniture, wanted to stand out in a 10' x 10'
space at the Kitchen & Bath Industry Show, they designed
painted backdrops with cartoon-style furniture on them. Actual
knobs were then mounted on the backdrops using grommets,
creating a surrealistic home. Hob Knobs owner Denise Harvey
says that in addition to being easy to install and transport, the
backdrops worked to generate lots of "buzz" for the booth.

Because the display cost less than $1,000 to produce, Harvey was
able to justify adding a kitchen scene and vanity to the backdrop
the following year.

of suntan lotion, and you've got a truly multi-sensory experience!

Get out of the box! Superior Communications wanted to create a relaxed atmosphere in the middle of a very high-tech cellular industry show. So they came up with the concept, "When you work with us, it's like R&R," according to Marcelle Greene, Superior's Vice President of Marketing. They decided to use two pop-up campers for conference rooms. From there, they built the theme, "Camp Superior," creating redwood trees with help from Jackson Shrub (a Hollywood prop company), a rock fountain (named "Lake Superior"), rustic trail signs and even an artificial campfire. They continued setting the mood with sounds of crickets and frogs, and the occasional coyote howl. Products were displayed on a clothesline hung between the trees, along with custom-designed Superior boxer shorts.

Creating an Experience

People remember:
- 10% of what they read
- 20% of what they hear
- 30% of what they see
- 50% of what they see *and* hear
- 70% of what they say
- 90% of what they say *and* do (more on this in Chapter 9: Impressing the Neighbors)

(Source: Dale's Cone of Experience)

The more senses you combine, the higher the retention rate. In addition, you are creating an overall experience for your visitors, much like the theme restaurant, Rainforest Cafe. Restaurant guests start by seeing trees and various jungle critters, hear ing the sounds of a waterfall and occasional "thunderstorms," touching all kinds of merchandise in the gift shop, smelling not only the food but also the mist from that waterfall, and of course tasting the food. If you've ever been to a Rainforest Cafe, just reading this description probably transported you back to your experience there. Isn't that what you want visitors in your booth to take away with them?

In the book *The Experience Economy,* authors Joseph Pine and Jim Gilmore offer examples of multi-sensory experiences from the world of retail. Just like successful retailers have found a way to make their products a part of the overall shopping experience, exhibitors can turn a passive experience (watching endless presentations on the show floor) into an active one. Pine and Gilmore suggest you start by finding a way to "-ing your thing." Instead of selling clothes, create a "wearing experience"; instead of selling stereo equipment, create a "listening experience."

Pine and Gilmore offer some basic keys to creating an experiential display. Start by keeping it consistent with your company culture. Don't design a stuffy, strictly-business booth if your company is known for a fun-loving nature. For a high-energy, cutting-edge company, use moving lights, upbeat music and animation. For a more conservative company, use softer lighting, soothing music and a display made with traditional materials in

 Basic Emotions Triggered by Scents

Happy = floral or citrus
Relaxed = vanilla or lavender
Increased energy = citrus or peppermint
Heightened productivity = floral or pine

Did you know? The sense of smell is one of the strongest memory triggers, reminding visitors of past experiences. People can be transported to another time and place just by smelling fresh baked cookies, a leathery new car smell, or a certain cologne.

Idea: Have an aromatherapy consultant in your booth as an attraction. Hand out scented oils that will help people relax and get to sleep in their hotel that night.

Caution: Don't let the scents get too strong; people can be very sensitive to fragrance.

classic colors. Create a story line (theme). Next, reinforce your theme and create an impression by using positive visual cues (props). Mix it all together with memorabilia (giveaways) and engage multiple senses. To be truly effective as an experience, your booth needs to alter the

 ## Using Theatrical Elements to Illustrate Abstract Concepts

Building on their theme of "The Elements of Networking," AT&T used the four basic elements of nature to illustrate why clients need AT&T as their networking resource during "turbulent times." Incorporating sight, sound and touch, they used the following techniques in their booth's theater presentation at several shows:

- Water: Video of dolphins, fish and the ocean were used to show the positive side, but then a storm illustrated what can happen when things go wrong. Visitors were sprayed with a fine mist.

- Fire: To illustrate being in the "hot seat," images of fire were combined with bench seats that heated up during the presentation.

- Wind: Attendees watched as images of a sailboat gave way to a tornado and the wind picked up, thanks to fans in strategic locations around the exhibit.

- Earth: To illustrate what happens when things fall apart, images of mountains crumbling in an earthquake were combined with rumbling sounds and shaking benches.

The presentation was used to guide attendees to the various demonstration stations, and produced a great response, according to Thomas Pearson, Marketing and Communication Manager for AT&T. The booth also won several awards.

attendees' sense of reality by creating a self-contained environment.

Engage them! Get them interacting with your product and staffers. People have short attention spans and are constantly bombarded with entertainment options and information. You have to combine education with entertainment and action. Get them involved in the presentation. Create photo opportunities in the booth. Ask for volunteers from the audience for demonstrations (more on booth attractions in Chapter 9: Impressing the Neighbors).

Designing So They'll Want to Buy

Your booth is your storefront. So think like retail owners, whether you are one or not! When you sketch your basic booth layout, make sure it includes:
- Good traffic flow (open, inviting design with easy entrance & exit; no barriers!)
- Product displays (clearly identified; include features & benefits)
- Adequate work areas (for presentations/ demonstrations, client conferences, lead collection, storage, etc.)
- Signage (appealing and informational with clear and definitive corporate identity)
- Lighting (creative and appropriate)
- Balance between hard surfaces (laminates) and softer elements (fabric or plants)

Did you know that plants can add life to your booth in more ways than one? Not only do they add character, but plants such as Peace Lilies, English ivy, Gerbera Daisies and potted palms can also help to remove indoor air pollution and chemicals, according to a study by NASA and the Associated Landscape Contractors of America. Using at least one plant per 10' x 10' booth can help with such common disorders as

> "Creativity is not just building a booth ... it's a total concept. You must create a unique approach."

> "Your display should match the personality of your company. If your audience is extreme sports enthusiasts, your display wouldn't work with mahogany wood paneling."

> - Harvey Hacker, Display Designs

headaches, eye irritation and respiratory problems. This leads to happier visitors and staffers. In addition, plants improve humidity levels, which can help preserve booth display materials.

So many times at shows, first glance down the aisles gives the illusion that the show is overcrowded with attendees. But as you walk the show, you discover that the real reason the aisles are full is because no one can get into any of the booths.

If your exhibit space is an island or peninsula, it must be accessible and visual from all sides.

Eliminate barriers – including the infamous six-foot table! For some reason, everyone thinks the only place it will fit is along the aisle. Not so! Rethink your booth floorplan. As the saying goes, "move it or lose it"! You've paid for the entire booth space, so make good use of it. There are no discounts given for using only the space along the aisle.

Don't try to fit too many things into a small space. If you have so many items to display that basic traffic flow is inhibited, then move up to a larger booth.

Get creative! At MacWorld Expo one year, Apple Computer reinforced their theme of "Think Different" by using a floorplan set on the diagonal. Attendees entered the booth through a long white open-area runway lined with all the various colored iMac computers. Combined with large overhead banners, the exhibit design worked to attract attendees.

The Language of Color

Color can be used to create a mood or reinforce corporate personality. The way you use it can make or break your exhibit. For example, if your company's main message is luxury, use sophisticated colors like black and gold. But if your message is fun and creativity, make your display kidlike with primary colors (red, blue and yellow), or tropical colors like bright pink and turquoise. Every color has a universal language of its own and sends numerous unspoken messages (both positive and negative), creating various moods.

 **Turning Lemons into Lemonade**

Big3D.com, a company who sells display murals, as well as lenticular (3D) and animated booth graphics, could have felt sorry for themselves when a large graphic panel met with an unfortunate puncture wound. But instead, they taped a sign over the hole in the panel saying, "Insert Forklift Here." It may have even helped to get them more attention!

Within each color, there is a range of shades, from pastels to grayed tones to vivid, deep colors. For example, within the red family you could have everything from pale pink to mauve to deep burgundy. Colors can also change based on how they are combined. A light color will look even lighter when contrasted with a dark color. Colors look even brighter when combined with black, or with complementary colors (opposites such as red with green, blue with orange, or yellow with violet). But keep in mind that using these kinds of color combinations can make your text very difficult to read.

Colors can be placed into two main categories: warm colors, which are high-energy colors that are highly visible and appear to advance or stand out; and cool colors, which are soothing colors that recede or blend in. The chart on the following pages shows what messages or moods are conveyed by the various colors.

The Language of Color

	Perceptions	Symbols & Meanings	Effects
Red (W)	Power color that commands attention; passionate, aggressive or dangerous; first color that babies perceive other than black & white	Fire, energy, blood (life); softer shades (rose or pink) considered sweet and feminine	Evokes a strong emotional response; raises blood pressure and stimulates the nervous system
Orange (W)	Warmest of all colors	Energy, playfulness and activity (appeals to the child in everyone)	Stimulates appetite; softer shades of coral and peach considered more sophisticated & relaxing (like a desert sunset)
Yellow (W)	Energizing and welcoming, cheerful and enlightening; can also indicate caution	Life-giving warmth of the sun	Commands the most attention when combined with black (think road signs & bumblebees)
Brown (W)	Earthy and wholesome, but can also be perceived as "dirty"		Deep tones of chocolate & coffee are associated with luxury
Blue (C)	Inspires confidence (often used in financial institutions); conveys authority and strength (police officers wear blue uniforms)	Hope, peace, honesty, responsibility and leadership ("blue-ribbon"); water and sky	Slows body's metabolism

	Perceptions	**Symbols & Meanings**	**Effects**
Green (C)	Fresh, renewing and comforting; conveys a sense of balance and productivity	Tranquility, nature, health and growth; also associated with money and prestige	Trendier lime green appeals to a younger crowd; bright emerald or rich olive appeal to a more upscale audience
Purple (C)	Complex color that blends the excitement of red with the calm of blue; youthful & contemporary	Whimsy & mystery; can be futuristic or high-tech; symbolizes royalty and authority	Can be over-whelming; best if used as an accent color
Black (N)	Mysterious, elegant and formal, yet sobering and strictly business	Independent; makes dramatic statement when combined with bright colors	Closes in a space and makes it seem smaller
White (N)	Minimalistic, brilliant and clear; can be seen as stark & sterile (soften with colored lighting)	Innocence and honesty	Makes a space appear larger; creamy off-whites are more inviting and friendly

One final thought on exhibit design: Even though your basic display should last for several years, your theme should stay fresh, not static! Don't reuse the same technique or theme year after year at the same shows. Rotate your theme. If it works really well for you, you may want to bring it back someday, but give it a couple of years' rest first!

Vocabulary

Backwall: a drape or panel along the back of a linear booth
Custom exhibit: a unique display built especially for a specific exhibitor
Double decker: a two-story booth; subject to special structural regulations
Graphic: elements such as logos, art or photos that enhance a display
Hardwall: a display built of wood or other solid elements as opposed to fabric or flexible panels
Modular: an exhibit made up of interchangeable elements or panels
Portable/Pop-up: lightweight units with collapsible frames
Prefab: a pre-built exhibit to be assembled in the booth space
Self-contained exhibit: an exhibit where the crate becomes a part of the display
Tabletop: a portable display that fits on top of a table

Booth Types

Corner Booth: booth at the end of a row bordered by at least two aisles; allows for more flexibility in booth design than an in-line booth
End Cap/Peninsula: booth with an aisle on three sides
Island: freestanding booth with aisles on all four sides; incorporates at least four standard booth spaces
In-line/Linear: standard booth in the middle of a row of booths with aisle access only in the front
Perimeter Booth: booth located along the outer wall of the exhibit hall (often the maximum backwall height is higher for these booths, since this would not interfere with any other booths)

Resources

ASCAP
www.ascap.com

BMI
www.bmi.com

Big 3-D.com
559-233-3380
www.big3d.com

Catalyst Exhibits
877-397-3682
www.catalystexhibits.com

Display Designs
800-220-3882
www.displaydesigns1.com

Jackson Shrub
818-982-0100

Transformit
207-856-9911
www.transformitdesign.com

Upstaging
847-949-4900
www.upstaging.com

**Underwriters
Laboratories (U.L.)**
847-272-8800
www.ul.com

Fictional Case Study: DigiCrayon

Scenario:

A small educational software company who wants to showcase their newest creation: a landscape design program, featuring an online gardening guide

Show:

Local Home & Garden Show, estimated 20,000 attendees over three days (28 hours); a horizontal consumer show

Exhibit:

10' x 10' booth

Goals:

Out of those who stop at the booth:
- Sell 250 software packages ($49.95 retail at a show special of $35; $8,750 total sales)
- Gather mailing list of 500 names
- Gain local media coverage (at least 2 stories)

Breakdown:

18 leads and 9 sales per hour

Budget:

$1,000	Space rental
$ 750	Booth design
$ 800	Show services
$ 750	Promotions
$ 400	Staffing
$ 300	Misc. expenses
$4,000	

Theme:

"Where Technology Blooms"

Booth Design:

- Use existing backwall graphic of a flower garden; blend potted plants (with "blooming" CDs) and a tree (with CD "fruit" hanging on it into the backwall
- Place an old computer monitor in the center of the backwall with plants growing out of it
- Include two stations (2' x 2' counters): one for demos and the other for lead management (with storage underneath
- Create an experience with sounds of birds, insects and water
- Add scents of flowers and rain

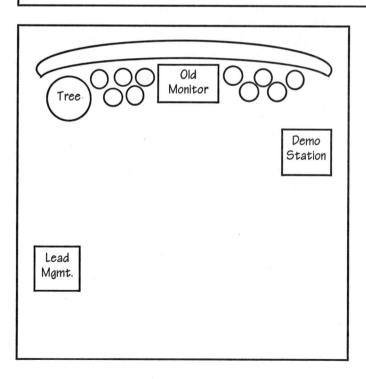

Fictional Case Study: Purple Carrot Press

Scenario:

A children's book publisher wants to showcase their new line of collateral materials (stuffed toys, games, puzzles); two main characters to feature: Sunny the Frog and Alyssa

Show:

Regional book and toy retailers' show with an estimated 7,000 attendees over two days (14 hours); a vertical trade show

Exhibit:

20' x 30' island booth

Goals:

Out of those who stop at the booth:
- Gain 550 leads (stores to possibly carry products)
- Sign up 100 new retailers within 30 days of show
- Gain media coverage (at least one TV and one print)

Breakdown:

40 leads per hour

Budget:

$10,000	Space rental
$ 7,500	Booth design & new graphics
$8,000	Show services
$5,000	Shipping
$6,500	Travel & lodging (10 staffers)
$8,000	Promotions
$2,500	Staffing
$2,500	Misc. expenses
$50,000	

Theme:

"More than Just a Story"

Booth Design:
- Use existing island display frame with new graphics (oversized reproductions of actual storybook pages)
- Four product display stations (with a mix of books and other items; connected to giant book with arches); each has storage underneath
- Incorporate giant puzzles on floor
- Create an experience with sounds of frogs and insects, or books on tape being played over product stations (using plexiglass sound domes)
- Add scents of grass for Sunny the Frog and tea party items (cookies, lemonade) for Alyssa

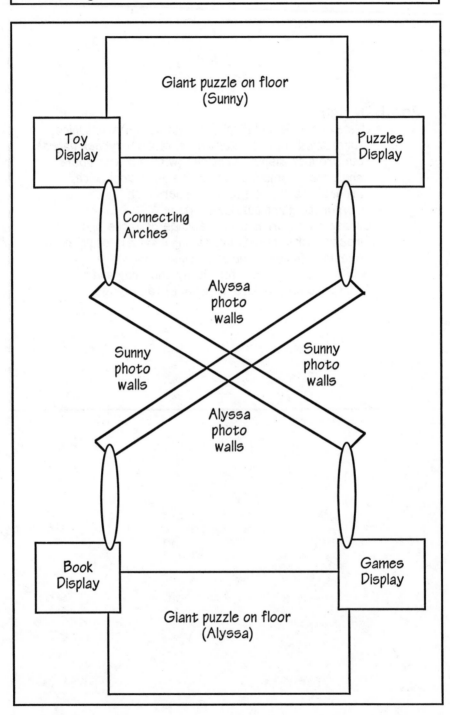

Finishing the Interior

Just like in the construction of a house, there's more to exhibiting than designing the exterior. Interior design (content) is where the "heart" of the project comes together. It should flow well with the exterior (booth design), in order to avoid conflicting messages, and to reinforce the theme.

Another vital, yet seemingly invisible, part of any building project is the wiring. If a house is wired improperly, it really doesn't matter how beautiful it is on the outside. It won't be functional.

In a trade show booth, the real power source comes from the people you choose to staff your booth, meeting and greeting the attendees. A poorly trained or unprepared booth staff can spoil an otherwise successful exhibit marketing plan. In order to get the power that you need, you have to ...

Generate Energy

Did you know?

➡ 85% of a visitor's overall first impression is based on the booth staffer, and that staffer also accounts for 80% of their final decision whether or not to do business with that company! (*Source: Various industry surveys*)

Do these statistics scare you? They should! Selecting your booth staff should be a critical part of your exhibit planning. Not only do you need to have adequate staff (see formula below), but you need to make sure you have the *right* staff. If you're going to a show where sales are allowed, it makes good sense to have salespeople in the booth. However, if sales are not allowed, have more product specialists or technical people on hand to answer a variety of questions – include members of shipping, quality control, manufacturing, and management.

> "You can dream, create, design and build the most wonderful place in the world ... but it requires people to make the dream a reality."
>
> – Walt Disney

Since a huge percentage of attendees at many industry shows are CEOs, company owners, vice presidents and other members of management, you should schedule times for your company's key executives to be in the booth. You could play it up by announcing the times in your pre-show promotions (much like a celebrity appearance), or even schedule VIP appointments with key clients and prospects.

Booth Staffing Formula

You must have enough staff to handle the traffic you expect, yet not seem overcrowded. Here's an easy equation to help you calculate your booth staffing needs:

Number of leads per hour
÷ Number each staffer can handle
= Number of staffers needed in booth
(Source: CEIR Report #MC1)

Example:

Leads per hour	24
Leads per staffer	÷ 6
Staffers needed in booth at all times	4

(With a maximum of two staffers per 10' x 10' booth space, this company will need at least a 10' x 20' space.)

Don't send your newest recruits to staff the booth. There just isn't room for the "learning curve." Definitely do not use trade shows as a "reward" for performance contests. Anyone who thinks trade shows are a vacation has certainly never worked one!

Criteria for choosing booth staffers

- Approachable, outgoing, people-oriented
- Professional; experienced at trade shows (understand how shows work)
- Comfortable engaging people
- Able to qualify before selling
- Knowledgeable about company and products
- Good communicator (clear, simple message)
- Good listener
- Enthusiastic (But you don't want someone who will "blow people away"!)
- Good attitude
- Familiar with competition
- Polite to "lookers," yet won't waste time

Remember:
Trade show sales are very different than field sales – just because someone is great in the field doesn't guarantee they will be successful in the booth. Train them!

Remember, your staffers are ambassadors for your company!

To Temp or Not To Temp?

Temporary staffers can be very helpful for attracting and greeting people, as well as doing some preliminary qualifying (more on that in Chapter 7: Finishing Touches). Hiring locally can also help to trim your travel budget. If you choose to hire temp staffers, look for experience, not glamour. Ask yourself if you would hire that person as a sales representative – which is basically what you're doing!

Be very specific when describing what is expected (including attire) and what their duties will include. You don't want any surprises the day of the show! After you've checked their references, send them product information so they can study ahead of time. Then meet briefly with them prior to the show to answer questions and do a "dress rehearsal" on <u>engaging</u> and <u>qualifying</u> visitors.

Is your booth staff a reflection of the attendee demographics at the show? Make sure you have some age and gender diversity when selecting your staffers.

Appearance

It's important to dress not only for your audience but also to reinforce your company's position and brand. Find out what the dress code is in the show city, as well as what's expected at the show. You may also want to dress according to your exhibit theme, using ideas such as:
- tuxedos
- Hawaiian shirts
- surgical scrubs
- sports uniforms
- military camouflage

One trend of the 1990s was for the entire booth staff to wear matching polos or oxfords, complete with company logos and/or web addresses

Staff Appearance

Hair: clean and controlled, not too long
Facial hair: neatly trimmed
Nails: well-manicured, polish optional
Makeup: professional, yet not overdone
Jewelry: tasteful and appropriate; nothing too large or gaudy

Instead of matching shirts, consider using custom ties, scarves or vests. Your staff will not only stand out, but they will also create more buzz.

embroidered on them. While this is a good way to establish a team identity, so many companies have gone this route that now the show floor is a sea of various colored polos and oxfords. And unless you have shirts that are custom-designed, you could end up next to a company with shirts the same color as yours!

As anyone who has worked a show knows, you'd better wear comfortable shoes! Standing for hours can really do a number on your feet, knees and back if you wear the wrong shoes. Some exhibitors even bring a spare pair of shoes to the booth and change midway through the day. It's amazing how that simple change can re-energize you! Another good idea is to use padding under the carpet in your booth. In addition to providing comfort for staffers, it also helps to keep prospects in your booth longer.

Remember, apparel is only part of the booth staff's overall appearance. Pay attention to details! Make sure all staffers are neat and well-groomed; clothing should be as wrinkle-free as possible and shoes neatly polished. Classy corporate attire can't overcome poor hygiene or sloppiness. Go easy on the cologne (some people may be highly allergic), and use breath mints after lunch, especially if having a deli sandwich with onions!

Also included in your overall appearance are your verbal skills, posture and manners. If you have staffers who seem to have trouble in these areas, either retrain them or choose someone else to staff your booth!

Booth Behavior

Once upon a Trade Show, there was an empty 10'x10' booth. About an hour after the show opened, two men appeared in the booth. They put up divider walls across the back and along both sides of the space, leaving the ugly backs of the side walls exposed to their neighbors, rising above the pipe and drape.

Slowly, the booth staffers began to appear, one...two...three...four...five! They all stood and chatted with each other, occasionally stopping to demonstrate their rather loud product, especially during presentations on the nearby event stage.

As the days went by, the staffers discovered ways to make the time pass. Two of them played cell phone tag, calling each other and blowing a whistle into the phone from various locations around the show floor.

After enjoying a dinner of chicken wings in the booth, they decided to play a game of Nerf football. Obviously, they needed the practice, since the football landed mostly in other exhibitors' booths. Fortunately, there was a big game on TV that weekend, so they were able to watch it in the booth on their mini-screen TV.

By the last day of the show, the staffers realized they were way behind on their goal of qualified leads, so they began to chase customers down the aisles, laughing, "Yes ... I'm following you! Hey, do you want to help me win a steak dinner?"

Believe it or not, this sad tale is not fiction. It is a true story of one company's exhibiting practices witnessed at one particular show. The exhibitors in this example made so many mistakes, it's hard to know where to begin! From

Always wear your name badge high and on the right. This way, people can naturally glance at it as you shake hands.

The 10 Commandments of Trade Show Booth Staffing

1) You shall not sit.
2) You shall not create barriers to traffic.
3) You shall not eat or drink.
4) You shall not accost people in the aisles.
5) You shall not talk to your co-workers (or use cell phones).
6) You shall not fill your booth with staffers.
7) You shall not put your hands in your pockets.
8) You shall not put out every piece of literature you have.
9) You shall not leave early (or arrive late).
10) You shall smile!

the start, they got off on the wrong foot by arriving late to set up. When they finally did arrive, they made a horrible impression on their neighboring booths, as well as on those attendees who were already walking the show floor.

The first job of any booth staffer is to be approachable and professional, making a visitor feel welcome. Face the front of the booth and stand near the aisle (but not out in it). On the show floor, you have to constantly adapt to people. Learn to recognize the basic personality types and how to relate to them. Be a chameleon! (More on this in Chapter 7: Finishing Touches.)

Study body language. Recognize when a visitor's attitude is positive (shown by open posture, good eye contact, and leaning toward the speaker) or negative (shown by crossed arms, lack of eye contact, or taking a step away from the speaker).

Make time at your pre-show training sessions for role playing. Let staffers practice relating to different types of visitors and situations. Teach them to "mirror" a visitor by doing what they do. For example, if a visitor talks fast, the booth staffer needs to talk at a similar pace. Keep in mind that it's not a race, but if you constantly drag behind, you will lose their attention.

Ideally, a pre-show training session should be held about a month prior to the show, in order to provide time to implement changes. Some good topics to cover include:

- Make booth assignments; limit booth shifts to three or four hours
- Assign a "Booth Captain" to facilitate any staffing issues, troubleshoot with show services, and be a media liaison
- Define goals and target market
- Outline behavior expected, as well as incentives (WIFM: "What's in it for me?")
- Review pre-show promotions
- Go over a list of attendee FAQs (Frequently asked questions) and appropriate responses

 Breaking Down the Barriers

Booth staff can become a barrier to traffic. How many times have you seen an island booth with staffers lining the perimeter? This "border guard" is certainly intimidating to attendees. Yes, your staff should be ready to welcome people into your booth, but spread them out a little. Don't ever let it look like you're waiting to gang up on attendees.

Assign duties to each staffer in the booth: greeting attendees, demonstrating product, qualifying leads, etc. Make sure they know how to help the customer make a smooth transition from one staffer to another. Also have "assignments" outside the booth: monitoring the competition, scoping out trends, contacting vendors and existing clients, etc. Assign certain aisles to each staffer to make sure that together you cover the entire show. Decide which staffers should attend which educational sessions – another great opportunity to learn and network!

Sales staff often object to any training because they already know how to sell. Wrong! The trade show floor is a whole different world. They won't have the luxury of time that they would have in a traditional field sales call, and need to know how to qualify, educate and close in a matter of fifteen minutes or less.

Did you know?

➤ Staff training can increase the number of qualified leads by 68%. *(Source:* CEIR *Power of Exhibitions* II) Without training, your staff could end up looking like deer in the headlights!

Booth Staffing Manual Contents

➤ Show hours and staffing schedule

➤ Set-up and tear-down details (including shipping procedures)

➤ Hotel and transportation information (incl. packing tips)

➤ Dining information

➤ Dress code

➤ Show floor plan with booth number circled

➤ Diagram of booth layout (makes set up easier)

➤ Pre-show promotions information

➤ List of items to display/hand out (literature & giveaways)

➤ Goals for show, as well as main message and theme

➤ Audience demographics; what makes a qualified lead

➤ Booth behavior tips/instructions for engaging and qualifying leads

➤ Lead management tips

➤ Basic product information

➤ Guidelines for dealing with press (also copies of all press releases sent)

➤ Description of any contests or special promotions (including hospitality events)

➤ Key company contacts (and contact numbers for all staffers at the show)

➤ Frequently Asked Questions "cheat sheet"

Not only should you provide pre-show training for your staff, but also hold team meetings each day of the show to communicate daily goals, report on results so far, and review techniques (such as engaging, qualifying, and overcoming objections). Create a booth staffing manual and give a copy to each staffer prior to the show (also keep a copy in your booth).

TradeShowTips Online
Issue #18: Trade Show Commandment #3: No eating!

This seems like such a silly thing to mention to professional adults, yet this is one commandment that seems to be broken often. And usually quite obnoxiously!

Once at a show in Chicago, as I was approaching a booth, I actually saw the man working it spit out his just-inserted handful of popcorn and make his way to the trash can before coming over to greet me. Needless to say, I didn't shake his hand! (Nor did I stay long in his booth.)

So often it seems that show managers almost encourage this bad behavior by scheduling a "reception on the show floor." Once this reception starts, many exhibitors somehow shift gears from "business" to "party." They often stand around snacking in their booth, totally oblivious to the attendees. It has now become a social event, not a business event.

Sure, you get hungry when working a show. But that's what breaks are for! Go grab that ice cream cone from the food vendors and pull up a seat in the exhibitor lounge. That way, you can rest your feet while you recharge your batteries.

Take Care of Yourself

- Take plenty of breaks (at least every two hours – walk around the show or find a comfortable place to sit outside the booth; give yourself a quick neck and shoulder massage)
- Wear comfortable leather shoes (so your feet can breathe), elevate your feet in the evening and apply lotion; don't wear the same shoes every day
- Stretch before going on duty in the booth and during breaks
- Remember to take deep breaths periodically to calm down and release stress; also watch that your posture doesn't become tense
- Drink plenty of water (also avoid caffeine and alcohol)
- Eat healthy, not heavy (fruit, turkey or ham sandwich, salad, steamed veggies, baked potato; avoid fast foods)
- Keep energy bars on hand (but don't eat them in the booth)
- Get extra sleep

Don't quit too soon. Maintain 100 percent effort throughout the entire show. Don't arrive late or leave early. And just in case you ever have the desire to pack it in halfway through the last day of the show, remember the following story.

At a "mega-show" in a major American city (details have been omitted to protect the guilty), an exhibitor decided that he would "just put away a few things that no one would miss" about four hours early. As he was gathering up these "minor" things, suddenly his entire booth went crashing to the floor! Luckily, he didn't have glass display cases and no one was seriously hurt, but can you imagine his horror? So much for nobody noticing.

Make sure that each staffer's family has a copy of their itinerary.

Tips for Frequent Travelers
(Source: Kathy Sudeikis, All About Travel)

Packing
- Choose luggage that doesn't look like everyone else's (or you can use colorful straps or handles).
- Create a packing list; plan your wardrobe in advance to allow time for any last-minute repairs or drycleaning.
- Keep mini-sized personal products in your travel bag, along with a duplicate toothbrush; also carry snacks (to save money on airport food).
- Take along $100 worth of crisp, new dollar bills – this makes cab fares and tipping a cinch! (But don't carry all your money around with you.)
- Carry a fully-charged spare battery for your cell phone, pager and laptop (be able to recharge them on the road).

Airlines
- Fly early in the day to avoid delays. If your plane is delayed or cancelled, call your travel agent first; he or she can tell you which other carriers will cooperate. The magic word to use at the ticket counter is "Rule 240," which means the original airline may bear the responsibility for putting you on another carrier to your original destination.
- See if the airport in the show city has a Web site and check it before you take off to be alerted to any problems, such as parking garage construction. If you can, sign up for e-mail updates.
- Check the Flighttracker.com web site for on-time arrivals.
- Always double-check airline luggage allowances.

Hotels
- Use the hotel's "Do not disturb" sign to keep your belongings more secure (no one enters your room while you're not there).
- Reconfirm the hotel's airport shuttle schedule. (Is it 24-hours?)

Car Rentals
- Ask if they have cars with a global positioning system (GPS).
- Write down your rental car's license plate number and your hotel room number. (Frequent trips and long days can make even the sharpest minds forget!)

Talk about being caught red-handed! DON'T let this happen to you. By the way, the exhibitor who related this story also shared that his best lead of the entire show came on the afternoon of the last day, long after the disaster across the aisle. Because you never know who is walking the show at any given time, don't take anyone for granted. They might be your next million-dollar account!

Vocabulary

Engaging: the initial interaction between a booth staffer and a visitor; needs to be open-ended and capture the visitor's interest

Qualifying: using pre-determined criteria to establish whether or not a booth visitor fits the target demographic desired

Fictional Case Study: DigiCrayon

Scenario:
A small educational software company who wants to showcase their newest creation: a landscape design program, featuring an online gardening guide

Show:
Local Home & Garden Show, estimated 20,000 attendees over three days (28 hours); a horizontal consumer show

Exhibit:
10' x 10' booth

Goals:
Out of those who stop at the booth:
- Sell 250 software packages ($49.95 retail at a show special of $35; $8,750 total sales)
- Gather mailing list of 500 names
- Gain local media coverage (at least 2 stories)

Breakdown:
18 leads and 9 sales per hour

Budget:
$1,000	Space rental
$ 750	Booth design
$ 800	Show services
$ 750	Promotions
$ 400	Staffing
$ 300	Misc. expenses
$4,000	

Theme:
"Where Technology Blooms"

Booth Design:
- Use existing backwall graphic of a flower garden; blend potted plants (with "blooming" CDs) and a tree (with CD "fruit" hanging on it into the backwall
- Place an old computer monitor in the center of the backwall with plants growing out of it
- Include two stations (2' x 2' counters): one for demos and the other for lead management (with storage underneath
- Create an experience with sounds of birds, insects and water
- Add scents of flowers and rain

Staff:
- Two staffers in booth at all times, one at each station

Attire:
- Khaki pants with floral or Hawaiian shirts

Fictional Case Study: Purple Carrot Press

Scenario:

A children's book publisher wants to showcase their new line of collateral materials (stuffed toys, games, puzzles); two main characters to feature: Sunny the Frog and Alyssa

Show:

Regional book and toy retailers' show with an estimated 7,000 attendees over two days (14 hours); a vertical trade show

Exhibit:

20' x 30' island booth

Goals:

Out of those who stop at the booth:
- Gain 550 leads (stores to possibly carry products)
- Sign up 100 new retailers within 30 days of show
- Gain media coverage (at least one TV and one print)

Breakdown:

40 leads per hour

Budget:

$10,000	Space rental
$ 7,500	Booth design & new graphics
$8,000	Show services
$5,000	Shipping
$6,500	Travel & lodging (10 staffers)
$8,000	Promotions
$2,500	Staffing
$2,500	Misc. expenses
$50,000	

Theme:
"More than Just a Story"

Booth Design:
- Use existing island display frame with new graphics (oversized reproductions of actual storybook pages)
- Four product display stations (with a mix of books and other items; connected to giant book with arches); each has storage underneath
- Incorporate giant puzzles on floor
- Create an experience with sounds of frogs and insects, or books on tape being played over product stations (using plexiglass sound domes)
- Add scents of grass for Sunny the Frog and tea party items (cookies, lemonade) for Alyssa

Staff:
- At least eight staffers in booth at all times, one at each product station and one at each "page" of the giant book

Attire:
- Men wear green shirts and black pants (to blend with Sunny's stories); Women wear rose shirts and black skirts (to blend with Alyssa's stories)

Finishing Touches

Why do so many staffers have trouble in the trade show environment? Because it's a lot like visiting a foreign country – if they haven't been prepared, they won't know how to handle the situations they are about to encounter. Combine this uneasiness with the natural human fear of rejection, and it's no wonder many staffers end up paralyzed with fear. It's easier to stand around talking with each other than to approach strangers. But you didn't pay all that money to talk among yourselves!

For a truly effective booth interaction, you need to know how to:
- Engage people with good opening lines
- Probe them to determine needs and qualify them
- Educate them by presenting solutions that respond to their needs
- Overcome objections that they raise
- Disengage by preparing them for the next step, or closing the sale

•➤ 55% of communication is based on appearance

•➤ 38% on tone of voice

•➤ 7% on actual words

(Source: Conselle Institute of Image Management)

Engaging

Knowing what to say to attendees takes some planning before the show. Don't wait for them to approach you, but don't shove brochures at people as they pass by your booth either. You're there to connect with them, not terrorize them! Chasing people or asking them to help you win a contest just doesn't work.

People buy based on relationships and trust first, then products or services. From the moment you say your first word, you're creating a chemistry that builds confidence in you, your company, and your products. Be customer-focused, not self-centered. Use appropriate eye contact to put people at ease and build rapport. Greet people and call them by name (but don't overdo it or you'll sound insincere).

Engaging should be brief – spend more time educating and probing.

Work at consciously listening, even if you don't agree or like what they're saying.

Working a trade show booth is not for the meek! You have to be able to get over your fear of rejection and be willing to start a conversation. Develop some good opening lines. (No, not like "Come here often?") Don't talk about the weather or ask if they want one of your giveaway items. Good openers:

- should be open-ended, not yes/no questions (think like a reporter: use who, what, when, where, why and how)
- must get the visitors talking about themselves or their company (interacting)
- need to draw them into the booth (attention-grabbing)
- are industry-related, product-related, or emphasize features/benefits

Probing/Qualifying

Once you get them started talking, LISTEN! Give them your undivided attention. You should spend 80 percent of your time listening to their needs, and only 20 percent of the time talking or providing solutions. Invite them to come in and take a look at your product. Above all, never ignore them or act rude or annoyed. The attendees are the reason you're there! Treat all people with respect, look them in the eye, and greet them with a smile. Offer them a firm, solid handshake, not a vice-grip or a dead-fish.

Ask the prospect questions about how they go about selecting products, what qualities they look for, and what their most pressing needs are. Find out about what they would like to accom-

Examples of Opening Lines

Question	Effectiveness
Can I help you?	**BAD** (easy to say no and walk away)
Enjoying the show?	**BAD** (yes/no question)
What brings you to the show?	**BETTER** (uses open-ended question)
What does XYZ Company do? (learn by reading name badge)	**BETTER** (shows interest and gets them talking about themselves)
How familiar are you with...?	**BETTER** (gauges their level of interest)
How many times have you wished you could (save time, save money, etc.)?	**BEST** (points out a product or service benefit)
Where do you (dream of traveling, see your .....)?	**BEST** (points out a need or product feature)
What are your most important needs regarding...?	**BEST** (gets them to share needs/concerns)

Active vs. Passive Visitors

Active Visitors: are responsive and talkative, ask lots of questions, appear genuinely interested

Passive Visitors: hold back, don't show any emotion, provides only one or two-word answers

plish, as well as what they're currently using. (But remember — don't run down the competition!) Know what criteria makes a prospect highly qualified and listen for cues.

As you continue the conversation, begin asking qualifying questions to determine their level of interest, buying timeline and budget. Ask their permission to take notes as you talk. This shows that you're genuinely interested in them — they won't object! You'll also want to find out if this person is the final decision maker, or if not, who else you need to contact (more on designing and using lead cards in Chapter 11: Weatherproofing).

Be on the lookout for "Leeches" (time-monopolizers), "Collectors" (of paper or trinkets), "Players" (who are only out to win a prize), or "Spies" (undercover competitors). All of these people can steal your valuable time. The more you know how to qualify visitors, the easier these people will be to spot.

Anticipate possible questions and have staffers practice how to answer them before the show. Teach staffers to avoid negative phrases.

Instead of saying:	Try:
"I don't know"	"Let me find out that answer for you"
"Just a minute"	"Are you able to wait a minute?"
"We can't do that"	"What we recommend instead is ..."

Acknowledge what they're saying to you by nod-ding, smiling and saying things like "I see" or "That's interesting." Learn to think like a reporter – pay particular attention to key points and details so you can address them later, but avoid making judgments.

Be conscious of body language signals – both yours and theirs. Make sure your posture shows you are open and friendly (don't slouch or cross your arms). Likewise, tune in to non-verbal clues from them. If they cross their arms or avoid eye contact, realize you're losing them and change the line of conversation. If they look at their watch, find a way to wrap things up. Mirror them. If they take a step back, you should too. Don't ever step in closer unless they do first. Doing so threatens their personal space.

> "You're not there to be qualified by the attendees, you're there to qualify them."
>
> - Brian Bailey,
> Exhibit Consultant

How NOT to Attract People to Your Booth
(Excerpted from: TradeShowTips Online Issue #14)

The staff at one booth literally took me by the hand and pulled me into their booth. Not wanting to be rude, I kept looking for a polite way to make my exit. But first I was trapped in what felt like a late-night infomercial. (Remember the "But wait! There's more!" routines?) Finally, after about five minutes of frustration, I let them scan my badge so I could leave.

Not surprisingly, their follow-up was equally as bad. Their local rep called and left a message that she was following up on my request for information, but didn't tell me what company she was with or where she got my name. I figured it out when the infor-mation packet arrived the next day with her name in the letter, which was addressed to "Mary Arnold." Now how did they get Mary when they actually scanned my badge?

Educating

Appeal to both sides of the brain: logical and emotional. Know the basic buying motives: increased profits, enjoyment, prestige, avoiding pain, or fear of loss. After qualifying them and listening to their needs, you should have an idea as to which of these motives they are focused on. Your job is to tailor your entire (brief) presentation based on what they've told you. If there's not a match, let them go!

The same approach doesn't work for everyone. Your goal is to find and make a connection with each prospect. Learn to recognize the four basic personality types. You can distinguish them by they types of questions and concerns they raise (as shown in The IDEA of Personality chart on the following page). Then adapt your selling techniques to each type.

> Don't prejudge based on <u>badge color</u>. Imagine every person you meet is wearing a sign that says, "Make Me Feel Important!"
>
> Get the dollar signs out of your eyes! Don't think only in terms of immediate sales.

Attendees are tired and on information overload. They won't remember half of what you tell them. Although they may appear to be interested when they gather your literature, keep in mind that about 65 percent of what is picked up will get trashed. *(Source: CEIR Report #MC34)* So only bring enough materials for about 5 percent of the expected attendees, and even then, don't bring your entire selection of full-color brochures. Scale down to one basic sheet that outlines the benefits of your product or service, as well as your contact information (including your Web address). If you must put out literature, mark it "Display Copy" and have people ask for a copy. You can always send the additional materials later. Besides, that gives you a reason to get their contact information!

You want to show, not tell. By getting them involved in your presentation, you're facilitating a self-discovery process. They will be more "sold" on your product if they can participate in a hands-on demonstration or write down some information. They will also be more likely to remember what you tell them. Another way to get them involved is to make a statement about

Guide to The IDEA of Personality

	In-Charge	**Dramatic**	**Easygoing**	**Analytical**
Traits:	Results-oriented	People-oriented	Security-oriented	Detail-oriented
	Born leader	Cheerful	Patient	Curious
	Competitive	Enthusiastic	Faithful	Instinctive
	Self-assured	Spontaneous	Dislikes change	Skeptical
	Daring	Sense of humor	Good listener	Perfectionist
	Impatient	Talkative	Avoids conflict	Controlling
"Hot Buttons"	Power	Status	Dependability	End result
	Time	Inspiration	Honesty	Proven
	Respect	Fun	Teamwork	Data
	Risk	Recognition	Harmony	Intellect
Main Focus:	Goals	Glamour	Feelings	Data
This person needs to be:	in authority	the star	reassured	right
And needs you to be:	to the point	energetic	relatable	detailed
Makes decisions:	quickly, without wavering	based on emotions	only after building a relationship	after very careful consideration
Communication Style	straightforward and factual	fast and excited	slow and relaxed	"20 Questions"

your product, and then ask, "Do you know why?" They will soon sell themselves on the benefits.

Instead of facing the prospect, stand next to them as you go over your brochure or portfolio. Just like you can remove barriers in your booth by moving tables away from the aisles, you can

Using Questions According to Personality Types

	In-Charge	Dramatic	Easygoing	Analytical
Engaging	"How important is it to you to save time?"	"How would you like to be admired by your peers?"	"What are you looking for in a ...?"	"What problems have you had with...?"
Probing/ Qualifying	"What are your expectations for this product?"	"Since I value your opinion, please tell me ...." "If money were no object ...?"	"How important is a money-back guarantee to you?"	"How does this compare with others you've tried?" "What other questions do you have?"
Closing	"When would you like your product delivered?"	"Can you see yourself using this when ...?"	"How comfortable are you with this plan?"	"On a scale of 1 to 10 ..." "Is there any reason why ...?"

break down a barrier by being a little more informal.

Focus on one issue at a time, and only give them the information they ask for. On the show floor, you don't have time to go into your whole spiel!

Overcoming Objections

Begin by acknowledging the objection and empathize with their concerns. Use the "feel, felt, found" method: "I'm glad you brought that up. I can appreciate how you feel. Many of my customers felt the same way, but they found that :.."

Ask questions to clarify and determine the true obstacle. Often, you'll discover an entire series of objections that are simply a smoke screen for their ultimate concern: fear, risk or cost. Treat each question as an opportunity; if they weren't truly interested, they wouldn't bother to raise objections.

 **Networking Tips**

- Have at least one meal a day with customers or prospects at the show (introduce people to each other).
- Wear your name badge at all official show events (but not outside, to keep from making yourself a target for criminals).
- Introduce yourself to speakers and other participants in seminars.
- Make a point of introducing yourself to strangers and use people's names.
- At receptions, keep one hand free and always shake hands firmly.
- After meeting someone new at an event, keep in touch – periodically send notes or clippings of interest.

Present alternative solutions. Ask, "If I could eliminate that problem for you, is there anything else holding you back?" If that's their true objection, you've calmed their fears. If there's something else bothering them, they will tell you that, too.

If you don't know the answer to their question, be honest and admit that you don't know. Never try to bluff them! You should know which other

Attitude: The "Secret Ingredient"

Working a trade show is hard work, but having the right attitude can make all the difference. Associate with positive people: Enthusiasm is contagious!

Watch what you say to yourself – you may be your own worst critic. When you have the right attitude, your facial expressions and posture will convey your confidence and draw people in like a magnet!

staffers might have the answer and bring them into the conversation. If that's not possible, write down the question and affirm that you will get back to them as soon as you have an answer. Then do what you say!

Closing/Disengaging

Instead of simply asking for the sale, offer a choice between two alternatives: "Would you like the red one or the blue one?" "Did you want to take it with you today, or should I have it shipped to your office?" After asking for an order, pause and remember: "He who speaks first, loses [the sale]." Assume the sale and know when to look away from the prospect and start writing to give him or her time to respond.

If you're not making sales in the booth, confirm with them what type of follow up they desire and how soon they would like you to follow up. Again, use "either/or" questions: "Did you want me to send you a catalog, or would you prefer to have a sales rep call you?" To close, ask a series of "yes" questions to lead them to a decision:
- "Were you impressed with our demonstration?" (Yes)
- "Did our product have the features you're looking for?" (Yes)
- "Would you like to have a sales rep call you next week?" (Yes)

Reinforce what the prospect can expect next. For example: "Bill is the rep for your area. I'll have him give you a call next week to answer all of your questions."

Know when to move on! Thank them for spending time in the booth, then use a handshake as a disengaging tool, followed by taking a step back. This is also the time to give them literature or a thank-you promotional item. No matter whether they become a customer or not, everyone deserves your respect. Be curteous and considerate of both their time and yours.

Never forget to put yourself in the attendees' shoes. Periodically step out into the aisle and observe. Watch how people react to the other staffers. Are they smiling or do they look like a caged animal trying to escape? If attendees look like they are pulling on a rope, let them go!

Everyone's favorite radio station is WIFM: "What's in it for me?"

Vocabulary

Badge color: some shows assign different colored badges to attendees based on categories such as exhibitors, buyers, press members, students, etc.

Fictional Case Study: DigiCrayon

Scenario:
A small educational software company who wants to showcase their newest creation: a landscape design program, featuring an online gardening guide

Show:
Local Home & Garden Show, estimated 20,000 attendees over three days (28 hours); a horizontal consumer show

Exhibit:
10' x 10' booth

Goals:
Out of those who stop at the booth:
- Sell 250 software packages ($49.95 retail at a show special of $35; $8,750 total sales)
- Gather mailing list of 500 names
- Gain local media coverage (at least 2 stories)

Breakdown:
18 leads and 9 sales per hour

Budget:

$1,000	Space rental
$ 750	Booth design
$ 800	Show services
$ 750	Promotions
$ 400	Staffing
$ 300	Misc. expenses
$4,000	

Theme:
"Where Technology Blooms"

Booth Design:
- Use existing backwall graphic of a flower garden; blend potted plants (with "blooming" CDs) and a tree (with CD "fruit" hanging on it into the backwall
- Place an old computer monitor in the center of the backwall with plants growing out of it
- Include two stations (2' x 2' counters): one for demos and the other for lead management (with storage underneath
- Create an experience with sounds of birds, insects and water
- Add scents of flowers and rain

Staff:
- Two staffers in booth at all times, one at each station

Attire:
- Khaki pants with floral or Hawaiian shirts

Opening Lines:
- "What kind of garden does your computer grow?"
- "When was the last time your computer looked like this?" (referring to the display)

Qualifying:
- Find out if prospects own a home, plan to do any landscaping, and have a computer at home

---

Fictional Case Study: Purple Carrot Press

Scenario:
A children's book publisher wants to showcase their new line of collateral materials (stuffed toys, games, puzzles); two main characters to feature: Sunny the Frog and Alyssa

Show:
Regional book and toy retailers' show with an estimated 7,000 attendees over two days (14 hours); a vertical trade show

Exhibit:
> 20' x 30' island booth

Goals:
> Out of those who stop at the booth:
> - Gain 550 leads (stores to possibly carry products)
> - Sign up 100 new retailers within 30 days of show
> - Gain media coverage (at least one TV and one print)

Breakdown:
> 40 leads per hour

Budget:

	$10,000	Space rental
	$ 7,500	Booth design & new graphics
	$8,000	Show services
	$5,000	Shipping
	$6,500	Travel & lodging (10 staffers)
	$8,000	Promotions
	$2,500	Staffing
	$2,500	Misc. expenses
	$50,000	

Theme:
> "More than Just a Story"

Booth Design:
> - Use existing island display frame with new graphics (oversized reproductions of actual storybook pages)
> - Four product display stations (with a mix of books and other items; connected to giant book with arches); each has storage underneath
> - Incorporate giant puzzles on floor
> - Create an experience with sounds of frogs and insects, or books on tape being played over product stations (using plexiglass sound domes)
> - Add scents of grass for Sunny the Frog and tea party items (cookies, lemonade) for Alyssa

Staff:

- At least eight staffers in booth at all times, one at each product station and one at each "page" of the giant book

Attire:

- Men wear green shirts and black pants (to blend with Sunny's stories); Women wear rose shirts and black skirts (to blend with Alyssa's stories)

Opening Lines:

- "When was the last time you played a game?"
- "Who's your favorite frog?" (Sunny, of course!)
- "How do you bring a book to life?"

Qualifying:

- Find out the prospect's type and size of store, target demographics, and who is in charge of buying decisions

"Structure is important, but only a part of the overall exhibit ... You should focus on 'audience acquisition' [with pre-show promotions] and learn to utilize existing materials in creative ways."

– Larry Emerson, MC^2

Landscaping

How many times have you noticed a beautiful house hiding behind atrocious landscaping, or perhaps no landscaping at all? There's not much inviting lookers to come inside when there's nothing to make that house stand out from a dozen other houses on the block.

Likewise, just because you've built a great booth doesn't mean the crowds will come! Why? Because your booth is one of dozens, probably hundreds, competing for their attention.

Often the biggest mistake exhibitors make is assuming that it's the show organizer's job to bring in the traffic. That's only partially correct. While show management should be promoting to bring people to the show (and if they're not, don't exhibit there!), it's your job to bring attendees to your booth!

This promotion takes three parts: personally inviting attendees, drawing people to your booth, and gaining media exposure (either before or at the show). You have to work at ...

Creating Curb Appeal

Did you know?

•→ Although 75% of attendees plan their visit to a show based on pre-show information, less than 25% of exhibitors are utilizing pre-show promotions to tip the scales in their favor! *(Source: CEIR Report #MC12)*

•→ Pre-show promotions can increase your booth traffic by up to 33% and raise sales conversion rate by 50%. *(Source: CEIR Power of Exhibitions II)*

Make Your Presence Known

A good pre-show promotion program can be a lifesaver if the show turns out to be a ghost town!

If you exhibit without doing pre-show promotions, it's like throwing a party and forgetting to send out any invitations. How do you expect people to come? You're just one of hundreds of exhibits in that huge exhibition hall, and guess what? Most of the people aren't coming just to see you! Somehow, you have to get on their must-see list.

Promoting your exhibit doesn't have to be hard. It can be as simple as printing stickers that say, "See us at booth #1001 at the XYZ Show on March 3 - 5." Then put those stickers on all kinds of materials you're currently using. Many show managers make the show's logo available for exhibitors to use in mailings. They may even have stickers available for you, but keep in mind that your message is more effective when it includes your booth number.

Speaking of show management, be sure to take advantage of other promotional opportunities they offer, including free or discounted show passes. You can send these out to your clients, VIPs or hot prospects. Also ask for their list of preregistered attendees, so you can invite those people to your booth as well.

So, who else should you contact? A good place to start is your current customers. A show is often an excellent place to have face-to-face contact with a customer that lives across the country, or even around the world. Exhibitors often hesitate to invite customers because their competition will also be at the show. Actually, a show is a great way for customers to comparison shop. Just do a great job showing them why they should continue to do business with you: Because you're the best!

Be sure to include current prospects, as well as prospects from last year's show who have not yet become customers. Maybe they just need a few

> People can't tell how big (or small) your booth is from your pre-show promotions, so make it look like yours is the place to be, even if you've got only a 10' x 10' booth!

 Types of Pre-Show Promotions

Mailers (most popular method)	Newsletters
Hand-delivered invitations	Telemarketing
Ads in trade publications	Broadcast faxes
Billboards/Banners	Web/E-mail
Coupons for "Show Specials"	CD-ROMs

Postcards (77% get read – CEIR Report #MC21)
"Lumpy mail" (package containing some type of gift along with the invitation)
Maps or restaurant guides for show city
Press releases (for more information, see chapter 10)

more questions answered before making their buying decision. When developing your list, be sure to weed out the least promising prospects and focus on your "hot list" first.

Creativity For All Budget Sizes

A suggested guideline for planning your promotions is to spend 10 to 12 percent of your overall trade show budget. But remember, the key is not in how many dollars you spend, but in how smart you spend them! Some of the most clever and memorable promotions can be done on a bare-bones budget.

The most effective pre-show mailers must be engaging and have a call to action. Do you want them to bring the card to your booth (this will help you track response)? Would you like them to visit your Web site to answer questions or enter a contest (which gets them interacting and exploring)? Give the reader an incentive to take action. Let them know what's in it for them to take the time to respond.

A relatively new type of pre-show promotion that is gaining in popularity is RewardMinutes prepaid phone cards. These cards are mailed out to prospects with instructions to visit your company's Web site to activate the card and qualify for a contest at the show. Then they must visit your booth to see if they've won. Two additional benefits of the program: Your prospect will hear your promotional message each time they use the card, and your sales force will receive immediate notification when a card is activated (allowing them to do timely follow-up, even before they get to the show), according to RewardMinutes' Andy Kovalinsky.

The average pre-show mailer pulls a response of 19%, and a hand-delivered invitation can gain a 41% response rate – far above the 1 to 3% of regular direct mail!

(Source: 1995 reader survey by EXHIBITOR Magazine, Rochester, Minn.)

Increasing Exposure

It takes seven exposures to your message before people remember.

3 Pre-show promotions/ads
1 Booth attraction/staff
1 Giveaway item with company info
1 Immediate follow-up
1 In-depth follow-up

Use the same graphic on your pre-show mailer that will be in your booth display. This increases recognition and recall when attendees see your exhibit.

Promotions That Work

Multiple mailings increase results. People need to see things at least seven times before they remember. (That's why TV commercials run so often!) The best response comes from two-part promotions, because people will have a stronger association between your promotion and your booth. Start by sending half of a promotional gift (the least expensive half) in your pre-show mailer. Then invite them to pick up the other half in your booth at the show.

Think clever! Create a teaser that intrigues them to come to the booth to satisfy their curiosity. For example, send a sunglass cord with the message, "Come to our booth and be dazzled by our new product. You'll also receive a gift with no strings attached ... except this one." At the booth, attendees receive the sunglasses to go with the cord. Another idea is to send batteries with the message, "Let us charge up your business," then give away flashlights at the show, suggests Lori Marshall, consultant with the promotional company Wood Associates. A pre-show mailer that includes a gift can double or even triple traffic in your booth. Not only is it more likely to get opened because it creates "lumpy mail," but it also creates anticipation.

The Logistics of Promotion

Your goal for all promotions, whether pre-show or in the booth, is to increase memorability, create positive feelings toward the company, and motivate attendees to purchase. If a promotion

 Good Pre-Show Mailer Examples

- Chicago Exhibit Productions sent a "Boarding Pass" for attendees to fill out and bring to the booth for a chance to win a weekend getaway. The card's copy fit with the theme: "We'll eliminate all the turbulence ..." and the questions helped to pre-qualify prospects.

- THINQ (an e-learning provider) designed postcards that were placed in the show registration bags. The cards asked, "Think you'd like a $100? We think so too." Attached was a green button that said, "Experience THINQ eLearning5." Attendees wearing the button on the show floor were selected at random to receive $100 by members of the THINQ Prize Patrol (one winner each hour).

- For the Superior Communications "Camp Superior" booth, the company sent a "trail map" of the exhibit floor with other exhibitors' booths marked according to the theme, such as "Nokia Flats," "Ericsson Valley," and "Motorola Mountain."

- Abex Display Systems sent a box with a close-up photo of a woman's eyes on the front bearing the caption, "Stare into these baby blues from point blank range and ask her ..." Inside, the thought finished with, "... if she'd like to arm wrestle." A shaker of "Arm Wrestling Chalk" was included. The promotion? To display their "strength," the company encouraged attendees to challenge the male and female World Arm Wrestling Champions, with winners receiving a free display system.

Negative Pre-Show Promotions

- Mailing a pre-show piece with no booth number (or show name!)
- Sending an e-mail with a Web link that doesn't work
- Getting prospects' names wrong, or sending to the wrong person at a company
- Using a mailer that was run off on a bad copier

doesn't perform in each of these categories, or if it doesn't fit with your overall theme, don't do it! A bad pre-show promotion can actually cause people to avoid your booth.

Timing your pre-show mailers is also important. There is a window of time before a show that is most effective. If you send your mailers too far in advance, people will forget. Sent too late, they may have their agenda already planned. If you wait too long, the mailer will be waiting in their mailbox when they return home from the show (or worse, arrive a week after they've returned)! If you can afford to do only one mailing, the best time to mail is two to three weeks prior to the show. You want them to receive it no less than four to five business days before they leave. If you want to do multiple mailers, start about 90 days prior to the show, then mail again 45 days out and about two weeks out. A good idea is to design a promotional calendar for yourself with mailing dates and media deadlines (more on this in Chapter 10: Becoming the Talk of the Town).

The cost of your mailing should be in proportion to the size of the potential sale. For example, if you sell a $10,000 product, you need a much more impressive mailer than if your average sale is $50.

More Pre-Show Ideas

Some other ideas for unique mailers that stand out from the crowd:

- Mini CD-ROM business cards that can contain text, audio, graphics or animation, Web links, and interactive games (produced by PreciseMedia)
- Custom key cards that are brought to the booth and scanned to discover if they've won
- Electronic invitations (E-vites) that are self-running animated "movies" with music or narration sent via e-mail; can use a tracking system to see who's opened and responded to the E-vite (created by MC^2)

 Direct Mail Tips

➥ Use a well-targeted list that has been checked for duplicate names and errors

➥ Mail first-class (even though it costs extra, it's more reliable and more likely to be read) and use stamps, not meters

➥ Don't use #10 white envelopes – Stand out!

➥ Use bulleted lists to grab attention

➥ Make the text visually appealing

➥ Use at least 9-point type in a serif font (vs. sans serif)

➥ Personalize – handwrite or type the person's name directly on the envelope or postcard

➥ Tease them with an envelope that begs to be opened ("What's in it for me?") and include the show name

➥ Use proven attention-getting words like: "announcing," "confidential," "discover," "easy," "free," "guarantee," "introducing," "learn," "love," "new," "powerful," "proven," "results," "safety," "save," "secret," "special offer," "trust," "you"

➥ Good wording: "Have you heard about ...." "10 Reasons Why ...." "Did you know that ...."

➥ P.S. – People always read a P.S.

- Talking swipe cards that announce when the card is swiped what prize an attendee has won (produced by Wood Associates)
- Three-dimensional pop-ups that mail flat, but are rubberband-activated when pulled from the envelope; designs ranging from a San Francisco trolley car to the Empire State Building or your own unique design (created by American Slide Chart)
- Lightweight video (or audio) tapes containing clips about your company or product and an invitation to visit your booth

---

 ## Be Your Clients' Travel Agent!

- Book a block of hotel rooms and let clients and prospects know all they need to do is confirm with you to reserve one.

- When they call to confirm, get their credit card number (for the room, so you don't get stuck with the bill) and set up their appointment time in your booth.

- You could also offer to arrange VIP ground transportation (limos or shuttles), restaurant reservations, or show registration (arrange with show management and you mail their badges to them).

- Promote a VIP lounge in your booth with Internet access or a business center (if you have a very large booth).

- Send them an appointment book with their time marked.

- What are the benefits for your company? You provide them with an added service, as well as gaining a confirmed appointment in the booth. Since you also know where they will be staying, you can arrange to have a welcome gift waiting in their room.

Resources

American Slide Chart
800-323-4433
www.americanslide
chart.com

**Bankers
Advertising Co.**
319-354-1020
www.bankersadvertising
.com

MC²
800-537-8073
www.mc-2online.com

Modern Postcard
800-959-8365
www.modernpostcard
.com

Reward Minutes
800-260-8825
www.rewardminutes
.com

Fictional Case Study: DigiCrayon

Scenario:
A small educational software company who wants to showcase their newest creation: a landscape design program, featuring an online gardening guide

Show:
Local Home & Garden Show, estimated 20,000 attendees over three days (28 hours); a horizontal consumer show

Exhibit:
10' x 10' booth

Goals:
Out of those who stop at the booth:
- Sell 250 software packages ($49.95 retail at a show special of $35; $8,750 total sales)

- Gather mailing list of 500 names
- Gain local media coverage (at least 2 stories)

Breakdown:
18 leads and 9 sales per hour

Budget:

	$1,000	Space rental
	$ 750	Booth design
	$ 800	Show services
	$ 750	Promotions
	$ 400	Staffing
	<u>$ 300</u>	Misc. expenses
	$4,000	

Theme:
"Where Technology Blooms"

Booth Design:
- Use existing backwall graphic of a flower garden; blend potted plants (with "blooming" CDs) and a tree (with CD "fruit" hanging on it into the backwall
- Place an old computer monitor in the center of the backwall with plants growing out of it
- Include two stations (2' x 2' counters): one for demos and the other for lead management (with storage underneath
- Create an experience with sounds of birds, insects and water
- Add scents of flowers and rain

Staff:
- Two staffers in booth at all times, one at each station

Attire:
- Khaki pants with floral or Hawaiian shirts

Opening Lines:
- "What kind of garden does your computer grow?"

- "When was the last time your computer looked like this?" (referring to the display)

Qualifying:
- Find out if prospects own a home, plan to do any landscaping, and have a computer at home

Pre-Show Promotions:
- Send series of postcard mailers
  - Mail to prospects and garden club list
  - Front of card has a photo of a computer monitor with a plant growing out of it (like what will be in display) and the message, "Discover the hidden garden inside your computer."
  - Back of card mentions show special (when they bring the card to the booth)
- Partner with local greenhouse to promote and provide plants for the display in exchange for signage and mention in promotions
- Place fliers at partner greenhouse and in local libraries

Fictional Case Study: Purple Carrot Press

Scenario:
A children's book publisher wants to showcase their new line of collateral materials (stuffed toys, games, puzzles); two main characters to feature: Sunny the Frog and Alyssa

Show:

Regional book and toy retailers' show with an estimated 7,000 attendees over two days (14 hours); a vertical trade show

Exhibit:

20' x 30' island booth

Goals:

Out of those who stop at the booth:
- Gain 550 leads (stores to possibly carry products)
- Sign up 100 new retailers within 30 days of show
- Gain media coverage (at least one TV and one print)

Breakdown:

40 leads per hour

Budget:

$10,000	Space rental
$ 7,500	Booth design & new graphics
$8,000	Show services
$5,000	Shipping
$6,500	Travel & lodging (10 staffers)
$8,000	Promotions
$2,500	Staffing
$2,500	Misc. expenses
$50,000	

Theme:

"More than Just a Story"

Booth Design:

- Use existing island display frame with new graphics (oversized reproductions of actual storybook pages)
- Four product display stations (with a mix of books and other items; connected to giant book with arches); each has storage underneath
- Incorporate giant puzzles on floor
- Create an experience with sounds of frogs and insects, or books on tape being played over product

stations (using plexiglass sound domes)
- Add scents of grass for Sunny the Frog and tea party items (cookies, lemonade) for Alyssa

Staff:

At least eight staffers in booth at all times, one at each product station and one at each "page" of giant book

Attire:

- Men wear green shirts and black pants (to blend with Sunny's stories); Women wear rose shirts and black skirts (to blend with Alyssa's stories)

Opening Lines:

- "When was the last time you played a game?"
- "Who's your favorite frog?" (Sunny!)
- "How do you bring a book to life?"

Qualifying:

- Find out prospect's type and size of store, target demographics and who is in charge of making buying decisions

Pre-Show Promotions:

- Send a series of mailers to clients and prospects
  - Mailer one: Postcard of Sunny the Frog
  - Mailer two: Postcard of Alyssa
  - Mailer three: 3-D pop-up "book" with a card invitation inside (with instructions to bring the completed card to the booth; also to save the pop-up for a surprise to come later)

"Tell me and
I'll forget

Show me and
I'll remember

Involve me and
I'll understand."

– Confucious

Impressing the Neighbors

Thinking of using a giveaway or other promotion in your exhibit? Before you plan your promotions ... any promotions ... you must ask: Who is your ideal customer? What are their interests or needs? If you're not focused on your audience, your promotions will fall flat. Good promotions will help you create excitement, build brand recognition, and qualify attendees. You want to make them remember you long after the show is over!

To Give or Not to Give?

There's a great difference of opinion among exhibitors as to whether or not to use giveaways. In some industries, it's either not practical or just simply impossible. In others, it's almost a given. In the book *The Experience Economy*, authors Pine and Gilmore call these giveaways "memorabilia" and compare them to souvenirs that people purchase on vacation to remember their experience.

Most companies stumble with the dilemma of what to give. First of all, the item needs to be useful, so attendees will want to keep it. It must be amusing and perhaps even trend-setting. If it has your company name on it, they might keep it – but if it has their name or photo, they'll definitely keep it!

> People won't remember everything you tell them, but they will walk away with the feeling you've created.

Some examples of the power of photos:

• At a Chamber show, the Kansas Speedway took instant photos of attendees standing next to their race car, printed them out, and made souvenir key chains on the spot!

• Sverdrup Civil Inc., an engineering construction firm, broke the mold at a conservative industry show by having Roadzilla in their booth, according to Jeanne Harwin. After designing a special costume, they hired an actor to dress up as Roadzilla and pose for Polaroids with attendees, complete with a Sverdrup label on the bottom of the photo. (And they accomplished all this in a 10' x 10' space!)

• InstaFotos creates custom photo postcards with the visitor's photo surrounded by views of the show city and name of the show. (They can also do custom mousepads, magnets, or photos in imprinted frames.)

 ### Want a Real Character in Your Booth?

"A costume mascot can represent a company with a friendly face or give a logo an identity," according to France Holland of Costume Specialists. These larger-than-life characters can attract crowds and enhance your company image. Expect to pay between $2,500 and $3,500, depending on the complexity of the design, Holland says. Additional fees include a one-time $500 charge to design a prototype costume, as well as storage, cleaning and maintenance fees. Can't swing a custom mascot of your own? Costume Specialists also has a variety of characters available to rent.

- Funny Faces can "morph" an attendee's photo (with their permission, of course!) and turn them into a "talking head" on the video screen. Each volunteer also receives a copy of the photo to take home.

Another advantage to these photo items? While attendees are able to get the item on the spot, it does take a few moments to produce. Voila! A captive audience for booth staff to present information about your company while they wait.

The best giveaways have three characteristics: logical, memorable and practical.

Logical:
- Does it fit with the theme of your booth and/or your company's marketing message?
- Does it make sense with what you do or sell? (A CD caddy for a software company, for example.)

Memorable:
- How unique or clever is it?
- Will it be remembered as being from you?

Practical:
- Does it have that "I gotta keep this on my desk" quality?

Avoid the "scoop & run" syndrome! Don't just pile giveaway items on tables – make attendees earn the gift. Offer it as a reward or thank-you for talking with a company representative, filling out a lead card, or watching a product demonstration. Always give quality gifts with high name recognition. Your goal is to leave a lasting impression, so make it a good one! If you use cheap gimmicks or cheesy trinkets, you may have created a company image you never intended.

> **Don't overlook samples of your own product as giveaways (if possible). That will certainly raise awareness with your prospects.**

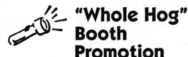

"Whole Hog" Booth Promotion

ELITeXPO plays off their ad campaign of avoiding shipping mixups, "No two hogs are alike" (the animal vs. the motorcycle), by giving away their "mascot," Eli T. Expo.

Eli, a pink stuffed hog in a leather jacket emblazoned with XPO on the back, comes complete with a tag stating his "birthday" and limited edition number, as well as company contact information. But a promotional item this nice can't go to just anyone looking for freebies! ELITeXPO prequalifies attendees using lead cards and awards Eli in periodic drawings.

Some examples of unique and clever giveaways:

• Compact, fold-away binoculars with the message, "Take a closer look at two great hotels in Chicago!" and logos of Sheraton Chicago and The Westin River North

• Interactive key chain with pushbutton sounds of seagulls for The Wildwoods Convention Center by the sea (this followed a pre-show mailer that announced "You haven't heard anything yet" and played the seagull sounds when opened)

• "Geek Pack": a plastic pocket protector containing a pen and a pair of black plastic glasses (complete with masking tape on the bridge!) imprinted with the company logo of BigEdison.com (a web design & hosting firm)

• "Prescription" filled with M&Ms with a label that says: "For fast, effective relief from planning headaches, take two tablets daily and visit www.EventSource.com" (a meeting planner Web site)

• Bean bag turtle with a tag providing facts about the sea turtles found at the Sheraton Sand Key Resort in Florida (They also handed out sand-filled key chains.)

• Disposable camera bearing the company logo (with the bonus of all photos showing the logo as well)

• Custom Magnetic Poetry sets with tiles that relate to your company

• Sandwich-shaped memo pads imprinted with your company logo; also available in cookie, burger, hot dog or waffle shapes – works great if you're using a food theme (from DeLano)

So how do you know how many items you'll need to give away? There's a delicate balance between too many and not enough. While it's always safer to overestimate (you can use the leftover items at a later show), you need to determine if it's worth the added shipping costs you might incur if you have several boxes to send back to the office. A good formula is to

 ## Recycling Trade Show Materials

Did you over-estimate the number of giveaways you would need? Don't worry! There's someone who will take them off your hands.

Network for the Needy was founded in 1990 as a part of the Professional Convention Management Association (PCMA), to assist with the donation of leftover food to charities across the country. Since then, the program has expanded to include promotional items (clothing, stuffed animals, office supplies, etc.) and literature, which are often donated to local children's shelters.

To get involved in this type of donation program, contact the convention center or hotel where the show is being held. Many convention centers are offering more traditional types of recycling (glass, cardboard, paper, etc.) as well. You can also contact PCMA for a complete manual of how the NftN process works and a list of participating venues.

start with the show's estimated attendance. Then look at how big your booth is (how many staffers you'll have) and the number of hours the show is open. Go back to your estimated traffic flow exercise in Chapter 1. How many highly qualified prospects do you expect to talk to? When in doubt, a good guideline is to bring enough giveaway items for about 5 percent of the show's anticipated attendance.

Should you estimate the ROI of your giveaway items? Certainly! You want to spend your money on the items that will get the most exposure for the money. A 25-cent pen probably won't get you much attention over the long run. A $5 or $10 item that will be kept on the prospect's desk, on the other hand, can be extremely effective. To get the best ROI, consider a high-quality

> **Survey people after the show to see if they remember receiving the gift and if they're still using it.**

Example: Figuring ROI of Giveaways

	Pen	Desk Clock
Item Cost	$0.50	$10.00
How many people will see it each month?	5 to 10	50 to 150
How long will the attendee keep it?	2 months	18 to 24 months
How many people will see it (total)?	10 to 20	900 to 3,600
Cost per impression (using the formula below)	$0.05 to $0.025	$0.003 to $0.011

$$\frac{Cost}{Impressions \ \times \ Repetition} = Cost \ per \ impression$$

item with the recepient's name on it. (Much like the power of photos!)

Low-Cost Promotion Ideas

- Have staffers wear "Ask Me About ..." buttons promoting your new product or service
- Fact booklets ("101 Ways to ...")
- Offer free consultations in the booth
- Free 30-day trial of your product or service
- "Show Specials": multiple purchase price; buy three, get one free; gift with purchase
- Hand out "tools of knowledge" or something that helps save people time or money (such as the Trade Show Manager's Planner or other calculators by American Slide Chart)
- Give gift certificates to encourage future business

 **Calling All VIPs ...**

Send pre-show mailers with various codes on them. Then have different giveaways for each target group, saving the best items for your VIPs or really hot prospects. Your booth staff will be able to prequalify a lead as soon as the visitor presents his or her card for the gift.

Just Say "No" to Fishbowls

Gone are the days of asking everyone who passes your booth to drop in a card to win a prize. Instead, the focus should be on getting them to interact with you. The idea of a drawing can be updated by having them bring their completed pre-show mailer in order to enter a contest. They've prequalified themselves!

Companies are increasingly using other methods to attract traffic. Chair massages, handwriting analysis, and caricature artists are becoming more popular. The benefit in each of these is that it provides you with a "captive audience" during the time the attendee is interacting with the expert or standing in line. This gives you an

Web-Based Promotions

Integrate the Web, both pre-show, at the show, and post-show. Tie it in with your pre-show promotions, driving traffic to your Web site and reinforcing your brand. At the show, take advantage of Webcasts to extend the reach of your exhibit. After the show is over, include photos of your booth (showing lots of traffic) and offer an incentive to again draw people to your Web site. Another bonus? People back home can see just how successful you were at the show!

opportunity to explain your product or service and do some qualifying of the prospect.

For handwriting analysis, have the writing sample relate to your company and print out the evaluation on your company's letterhead. Robin Olsen of Allied Van Lines says that their handwriting analysis expert has done an excellent job of attracting people at their booth. The expert helps to qualify visitors while talking with them about their handwriting.

Providing a massage station helps to build goodwill toward a company, according to Gary Buzzard of 20-Minute Vacation. It makes attendees feel good by easing tense muscles and enhancing circulation, a definite benefit for any weary visitor at a trade show. But it works best when most people at the show are potential customers, Buzzard cautions. In order to maximize the promotion, you should make sure people make the connection to your company. One way is to create graphics and signage that convey the message, "Let us take the stress out" or "Rest easy with XYZ Company."

One often overlooked promotional tool is the company description in the show program. It should serve as a teaser, telling attendees why they want to come to your booth. If you're using a special theme or attraction, mention that in your description so attendees will know when they've arrived at your booth. You can also take advantage of opportunities to advertise in the show directory and special editions of related trade publications.

Make your booth an attraction!

To truly create an immersive exhibit experience, start by asking what basic message you want your audience to walk away with, and then use some kind of attraction to create energy and excitement and bring your message to life. After all, exhibiting is selling in 3-D! Formulate your presentation so everything works together to reinforce your brand, but don't be too blatant about it.

1. Host a live theater presentation.

Susan Ossim of Jack Rouse Associates, a communications firm, says the goal of any presentation is "to create a sensory connection for

---

At-Show Promotions and Sponsorships

Most shows provide a myriad of opportunities to showcase your company besides a basic booth. For example, you may be able to sponsor the keynote speaker or an after-hours reception. (For more details on sponsorships, see Chapter 13: More than Selling Real Estate.)

Some other examples:

- Banners (show hall, hotel, or airport)
- Hotel closed-circuit TV channel
- Kiosks at show (such as exhibitor locators)
- Signage on shuttles/buses/taxis
- Hotel "door drops" (gifts dropped off at attendees' hotel rooms)
- Hospitality events (see more in Chapter 14: Housewarmings)
- Press kits/press conference (see more in Chapter 10: Becoming the Talk of the Town)

Increasing Booth Traffic

Studies show that booth attraction increases with:

Show sponsorships	104%
Hospitality events	86%
Press conferences	77%
Advertising	46%

(Source: CEIR Power of Exhibitions II)

instantaneous recall." This can be accomplished by having a catch phrase which is repeated throughout the presentation, putting the message to music, or tying the presentation in with your giveaway item. (JRA uses the slogan "Attract, Engage, Communicate.")

Like your booth design, your presentation style needs to fit with your message and corporate personality. Should it be wild and crazy or sleek and sophisticated? Keep it relevant, memorable and simple. You want to entertain, educate and create emotion by totally encompassing the audience in your message and producing an immediate response. Never do a presentation just for the entertainment value or "eye candy" alone (such as glamourous models or Vegas-style shows).

One of the benefits of a live presentation is that it creates one-on-one attention, while telling your story the way you want it told. Done right, a presentation helps to qualify the audience and makes them stick around afterwards to ask questions. Have staffers standing around the perimeter of the audience to keep from losing any hot prospects.

Get the audience involved; the more interactive the presentation, the more memorable it will be. Have the audience shout out answers to questions posed by the presenter, or respond to predetermined cues (like shouting "XYZ rocks!" every time a specific feature or product is mentioned). Another way to connect with the audience is to have an "audience advocate" or volunteer who goes up on stage with the presenter to demonstrate the product, recommends Denise Moyer of Flying Beyond, a marketing communications company.

It all starts with a good script, and then visuals are added to enhance the message, says Moyer. Do your homework by meeting the needs of the audience and making the message flow from that. Your goal should be to remove any preconceptions and get them ready for the next experience in your booth, whether that is a hands-on demonstration or talking to a salesperson.

Another benefit of live presentations are that they help create buzz for your company on the show floor. Of course, this works to your benefit only if the attendees remember not just the presentation, but are also able to recall the name of your company.

Presentations should always respect attendees' time. Stick to two or three main points. The experts recommend about a seven-minute presentation which is repeated often (about four times each hour). To avoid the theater area appearing dead between presentations, Moyer recommends to always have something playing on the video screen, like a countdown clock or teasers for the next presentation (movement attracts attention). Booth staffers can work as crowd gatherers and coax people to come in and sit down.

To incorporate a presentation into your booth, design a stage area, perhaps slightly elevated, and provide adequate distance between seats (approximately 24-inch diameter). Experts recommend a minimum 20' x 20' booth size to handle live presentations, but Moyer says it can be done in a 10' x 20' space (although it's challenging and has very limited seating). If you don't

> **"Less is more! You want people to be intrigued and drawn over for more information."**
>
> -Brian Bailey, Exhibit Consultant

have someone within your company who is an expert presenter, consider hiring a professional.

2. Conduct product demonstrations.

> Don't simply aim to be outrageous – you want to be memorable for your message and your product.

While a product demo won't draw the kind of crowd that a live theater presentation will, it can still help start a conversation. Don't get too technical – focus on benefits and use real-world examples. Maintain eye contact with the audience and again, keep it interactive. You can also withhold your giveaway item to give away after the demonstration. End with a "next step" call to action, like encouraging audience members to fill out a lead card or talk with a salesperson.

3. Find a celebrity or sports figure to interact with attendees, sign autographs, or pose for photos. (If you can't afford the real thing, hire a celebrity look-alike.)

• The Atlanta Convention & Visitors Bureau has used some unique attractions in their booth

Attention-Getting Tools

Virtual reality/Multimedia
Live presentations
Corporate illusionist
Press conference/Media gala
Hospitality function
In-booth giveaways
Photo opportunities
Demonstrations/Simulations
Celebrities or look-alikes

Show specials
Interactivity
Contests
Sponsorships
Massage
Shoe shine

as well. Rick Myers says that once, they were fortunate to have Butterfly McQueen from "Gone With the Wind" in the booth to sign autographs, along with Rhett and Scarlett look-alikes. Together, the trio gathered a lot of attention. At another show just before the 1996 Olympics, they created a news station look, complete with camera, and interviewed attendees who came to the booth.

• Nabisco's Michael Falkowitz says, "We believe in keeping it fun and lively and keeping the attendees involved." Their in-booth promotions have included a Major League Baseball tie-in, complete with ex-players in the booth.

• Abex Display Systems hosted the male and female World Arm Wrestling Champions in their booth to take on willing challengers.

• The Gale Group played off of their role as a research authority for the "Win Ben Stein's Money" game show by creating "Win Ben Stein's Undying Respect" at a show for librarians. Throughout most of the show, the game featured an animated version of the host (using his actual voice). But for a couple of hours one day, Stein appeared in person. "This was probably the most effective trade show promotion we've ever done," said Beth Dempsey. "He pretty much cleared the [rest of the exhibit hall] during his performance."

• Hire a "heckler"! Michael Pasternak will interrupt your spokesperson, dressed as Lt. Columbo, and ask a barrage of inane questions. This way, you can address the issues that you know the audience is thinking. It's another way to create an "audience advocate" and drive home your message.

> "Companies stage an experience when they engage customers in a memorable way ... Staging experiences is not about entertaining customers; it's about engaging them."
>
> – From **The Experience Economy**, by Joseph Pine & James Gilmore

• Host a booksigning for an author in your industry (if possible, sell the books in the booth – many publishers have quantity discounts available).

One word of caution when using celebrities: Be sure you work the line! Having a big name in your booth is bound to draw lots of people who may not necessarily become clients. Have staffers act as line managers to interview and qualify those waiting.

Working with Celebrities

•• Discuss fees early on in the process

•• Be prepared for special riders to your contract and get it spelled out up front (for travel expenses, lighting, labor, etc.)

•• Be prepared for all kinds of unusual requests (wants a specific color dressing room or will only drink one brand of bottled water)

•• Obtain the celebrity's permission before using their name in marketing materials

•• Check with the celebrity to see whether or not photos or videos are allowed

•• Determine what the celebrity's attire will be

•• Verify all travel arrangements

•• Assign a staff member to be a personal assistant for the celebrity

•• Allow the celebrity frequent breaks during the event

•• Be prepared to pay $25,000 or more – really big names can cost over $100,000!

•• To save money, utilize local talent (especially if the show is in Las Vegas, Nashville, etc.) or consider piggybacking with another group meeting the same week (check with the CVB or hotel)

Comparing Booth Attraction Types

	Pros	Cons	Examples
One-on-One	Workable in a 10' x 10' booth space	Must qualify each person as you go	Contest registration
	Informal; can easily be personalized for each attendee's needs	Requires a lot of time for each presentation	Product information kiosks
	Any staffer with good product knowledge can present		
Small Group	Workable in a 10' x 20' booth space	Crowd may get too large for each person to see	Interactive product demonstrations
	Can pre-qualify the group before meeting one-on-one with hot prospects	Requires a skilled presenter with extensive product knowledge	Traffic generators (magicians, massage stations, etc.)
Live Theater	Can pre-qualify lots of people at once	Expensive; requires a professional presenter	Multimedia, virtual reality, game shows
	Generate audience interaction	Takes up lots of space (min. 20' x 20' booth)	Celebrities or look-alikes

4. Design an interactive demonstration. (cooking, "make & takes", demo software, etc.).

• Dersé Exhibits held a "build your own booth" design contest in their booth at the Exhibitor Show in Las Vegas. Attendees took a 7-inch tile and built whatever came to mind with all kinds of trinkets and gizmos provided. Resulting creations were judged at the end of the show and digital photos were taken of the entries. Dersé's Jon Horn says the activity produced approximately 30 to 40 percent more leads than the previous year. Not only did attendees interact with staffers and each other, but they were also drawn back repeatedly to the booth to see the new creations.

• For consumer show exhibits, consider having how-to demonstrations or "make & takes," especially for kids.

5. Virtual reality theater or games

With technology constantly evolving in this area, there is an abundance of ideas to choose from: VR headsets, simulators (racing or sports), 3-D animation (à la the Wizard from the Wizard of Oz), and more. But be careful not to use technology just for the sake of the technology! Your booth attraction must relate to or enhance your core message.

Using a Virtual Reality theater can not only draw people to your booth and prequalify them, but also totally immerses them in your message using both sight and sound. In fact, Ham on Rye Technologies, designers of a patented VR system that utilizes a live presenter in a virtual world, has discovered that 95 percent of people will remember the exhibitor with the theater , with about 50 percent remembering at least part of

> While video walls and kiosks can work well to attract people, they won't necessarily help to qualify anyone. So use them as only one part of your overall presentation.

the message ... one year later! "It's cool and it's fun, and they're learning whether they like it or not," says Russell Kroeker, Director of Ham on Rye's Trade Show Division.

At these interactive presentations, attendees qualify themselves by answering questions (which Ham on Rye has customized for that exhibitor) on an electronic keypad. Booth staffers can see the answers immediately and know who are the hottest prospects by the time the presentation ends. With several people waiting their turn, staffers can work the line. In addition, there's no time wasted on those who aren't qualified. And Kroeker points out that by using customized questions exhibitors can help to prove their ROI on the exhibit.

When Vail Resorts wanted to introduce their out-of-bounds skiing experience at Denver's Snow Sports Expo, they used a virtual reality theater created by Ham on Rye. To promote the theater, they distributed tickets in the Denver Post. The results? Vail Resorts found themselves "the" destination at the show! The theater was filled all four days, with as many as 50 people waiting in line. An estimated 4,000 people were exposed to their message. They also received local radio and TV coverage.

Other ideas for interactive presentations:

• Audience polling has become a popular way for exhibitors to educate attendees about their products. Participants compete against each other by answering targeted questions about the company. Another favorite attention-getter is interactive trivia games (modeled after popular game shows).

Know the show rules regarding acceptable sound levels, costume restrictions, approved food vendors, and more. You don't want any surprises!

Don't become so "attractive" that you cause congestion in the aisles or you will be cited by show management!

• Jack Rouse Associates created a "Whac-a-Mole"-style game for a computer company called "Beat Server Downtime." The game demonstrated how the company's server eliminated downtime. Susan Ossim reports it was a huge success!

If you look like you're having fun, you will attract more people!

More in-booth attraction ideas:

- Treasure chest with keys (staff dressed as pirates)
- "Open the Door" with key card to insert (non-winning cards entered in a drawing)
- Magician or other entertainer who incorporates your product message into performance (such as Chef Anton, professional trick shot pool champion)
- Show specials (gives sense of urgency)
- Plasma screens or video walls
- Touch-screen kiosks
- Plexiglass sound domes over various stations
- ViewMaster custom reels (www.customviewmaster.com)

Lasting Impressions

When you're thinking creative with your promotions, never forget the real reason you're at the show is to create a memory in the attendees' minds. You want to be the one booth that they think about when they're back at the office.

Vocabulary

Sponsorships: opportunites other than booth space to showcase your company or product; offered by Show Management

Resources

American Slide Chart
800-323-4433
www.americanslidechart
.com

**Bankers
Advertising Co.**
319-354-1020
www.bankersadvertising
.com

Baskow & Associates
702-733-7818
www.baskow.com

Costume Specialists
614-464-2115

DeLano Service Inc.
800-748-0318
www.delanoservice.com

Flying Beyond
408-266-3220
www.fbeyond.com

**Funny Faces/Tracy Evans
Productions**
888-223-8669
www.tracyevans
productions.com

Ham on Rye
636-458-3232
www.hamonrye.com/
tradeshows

InstaFotos
650-571-9320
www.instafotos.com

Jack Rouse Associates
800-733-2025
www.jackrouse.com

Magnetic Poetry
800-370-7697
www.magneticpoetry
.com/Custom/
custom2.html

**Network for the Needy
(PCMA)**
312-423-7262
www.pcma.org

Network Music
800-854-2075
www.privatelabelcd
.com

Pasternak & Associates
818-716-5977

Wood Associates
408-965-4996
www.woodteam.com

Tricks of the Trade
(Chef Anton)
800-679-3859
www.chefanton.com

20-Minute Vacation
877-353-9114
www.20-minute
vacation.com

Fictional Case Study: DigiCrayon

Scenario:

A small educational software company who wants to showcase their newest creation: a landscape design program, featuring an online gardening guide

Show:

Local Home & Garden Show, estimated 20,000 attendees over three days (28 hours); a horizontal consumer show

Exhibit:

10' x 10' booth

Goals:

Out of those who stop at the booth:
- Sell 250 software packages ($49.95 retail at a show special of $35; $8,750 total sales)

- Gather mailing list of 500 names
- Gain local media coverage (at least 2 stories)

Breakdown:

18 leads and 9 sales per hour

Budget:

$1,000	Space rental
$ 750	Booth design
$ 800	Show services
$ 750	Promotions
$ 400	Staffing
$ 300	Misc. expenses
$4,000	

Theme:

"Where Technology Blooms"

Booth Design:

- Use existing backwall graphic of a flower garden; blend potted plants (with "blooming" CDs) and a tree (with CD "fruit" hanging on it into the backwall
- Place an old computer monitor in the center of the backwall with plants growing out of it
- Include two stations (2' x 2' counters): one for demos and the other for lead management (with storage underneath
- Create an experience with sounds of birds, insects and water
- Add scents of flowers and rain

Staff:

- Two staffers in booth at all times, one at each station

Attire:

- Khaki pants with floral or Hawaiian shirts

Opening Lines:
- "What kind of garden does your computer grow?"
- "When was the last time your computer looked like this?" (referring to the display)

Qualifying:
- Find out if prospects own a home, plan to do any landscaping, and have a computer at home

Pre-Show Promotions:
- Send series of postcard mailers
  - Mail to prospects and garden club list
  - Front of card has a photo of a computer monitor with a plant growing out of it (like what will be in display) and the message, "Discover the hidden garden inside your computer."
  - Back of card mentions show special (when they bring the card to the booth)
- Partner with local greenhouse to promote and provide plants for the display in exchange for signage and mention in promotions
- Place fliers at partner greenhouse and in local libraries

Attractions:
- Software demo (hands-on) as well as virtual-to-real photo transitions on screen

Giveaways:
- Printout of an attendee's basic design (allowing only 2 to 3 minutes each so they can't do a complete design)
- CD jewel case with flower-shaped CD demo (very limited; include virtual-to-real photos), promotional catalog of other software
- A seed packet (provided by the partner greenhouse)

Fictional Case Study: Purple Carrot Press

Scenario:

A children's book publisher wants to showcase their new line of collateral materials (stuffed toys, games, puzzles); two main characters to feature: Sunny the Frog and Alyssa

Show:

Regional book and toy retailers' show with an estimated 7,000 attendees over two days (14 hours); a vertical trade show

Exhibit:

20' x 30' island booth

Goals:

Out of those who stop at the booth:
- Gain 550 leads (stores to possibly carry products)
- Sign up 100 new retailers within 30 days of show
- Gain media coverage (at least one TV and one print)

Breakdown:

40 leads per hour

Budget:

$10,000	Space rental
$ 7,500	Booth design & new graphics
$8,000	Show services
$5,000	Shipping
$6,500	Travel & lodging (10 staffers)
$8,000	Promotions
$2,500	Staffing
$2,500	Misc. expenses
$50,000	

Theme:
"More than Just a Story"

Booth Design:
- Use existing island display frame with new graphics (oversized reproductions of actual storybook pages)
- Four product display stations (with a mix of books and other items; connected to giant book with arches); each has storage underneath
- Incorporate giant puzzles on floor
- Create an experience with sounds of frogs and insects, or books on tape being played over product stations (using plexiglass sound domes)
- Add scents of grass for Sunny the Frog and tea party items (cookies, lemonade) for Alyssa

Staff:
- At least eight staffers in booth at all times, one at each product station and one at each "page" of the giant book

Attire:
- Men wear green shirts and black pants (to blend with Sunny's stories); Women wear rose shirts and black skirts (to blend with Alyssa's stories)

Opening Lines:
- "When was the last time you played a game?"
- "Who's your favorite frog?" (Sunny, of course!)
- "How do you bring a book to life?"

Qualifying:
- Find out the prospect's type and size of store, target demographics, and who is in charge of buying decisions

Pre-Show Promotions:
- Send a series of mailers to clients and prospects
  - Mailer one: Postcard of Sunny the Frog

- Mailer two: Postcard of Alyssa
- Mailer three: 3-D pop-up "book" with a card invitation inside (with instructions to bring the completed card to the booth; also to save the pop-up for a surprise to come later)

Attractions:
- Costumed characters of Sunny the Frog and Alyssa on hand in the booth (alternating 20 minutes on and off) to pose for photos with attendees in front of the giant book
- One product station demonstrating the new Sunny game, with attendees encouraged to participate
- Special offer: Opportunity to host costume character in the client's store with a $1,000 wholesale order placed within 30 days of the show

Giveaways:
- Photos (fit in pre-show mailer pop-up book as frame)
- Drawing for $500 of bonus merchandise (using pre-show lead cards)

"All I know
is just what
I read in
the papers."

— Will Rogers

Becoming the Talk of the Town

When you're promoting your presence at a show, why do it all alone? By sending advance information to the appropriate media, you could find your company the subject of a feature article — not a bad way to create buzz!

Before you even think about contacting a reporter or editor, you need to develop a comprehensive media plan. Research your industry (or local area, for a consumer show) and determine what publications you should include in your media list. Find out from Show Management early on which publications do pre-show editions. Visit each publication's web site or call to find out deadlines and which reporters will be covering the show. For magazines, the deadline for the pre-show issue could be three to four months before the show.

Did you know?

•• In the United States there are:
>   12,230 newspapers
>   14,098 magazines
>   1,418 television stations
>   1,494 cable stations
>   9,628 radio stations

•• There are 9,559 professional and trade publications. (*Source: Gale Database of Publications & Broadcast Media, published by the Gale Group, Farmington Hills, Mich.*)

Work with Show Management to promote your exhibit. Find out if they are doing any pre-show press releases or press kits that you can be included in. Also find out about media relations at the show — will they have a Press Room available or other ways to distribute your information?

Press Release Tips

Successful press releases need to be:

•➤ Timely

•➤ Credible

•➤ Well-written (use the Associated Press Style Manual)

•➤ Concise (maximum of two pages, double-spaced)

•➤ Focused on a unique news angle

•➤ Relevant to each publication's readers or viewers (targeted for each audience; consumer vs. trade)

Time your release to arrive on Tuesday, Wednesday or Thursday.

Don't ever fax releases unless you've been told to do so.

Many people are unaware how much of the news comes from companies or public relations agencies contacting reporters. When done correctly, reporters don't mind receiving press releases – in fact, it helps them do their jobs of gathering news. But cross the line from genuine news to a self-promoting, thinly disguised ad, and you might as well kiss any hopes for media coverage good-bye.

Once you've defined your media targets, what should you send them? The most common tool used is the press release.

Writing a Release that's Newsworthy: "Just the Facts, Ma'am"

Each press release should have only one focal point, or "news peg." Not all releases need to be what's known as "hard news" (straightforward facts about a new product or event); many successful releases are written as a human interest or feature story. Either way, never include opinions (unless you're quoting someone, and all quotes must be attributed to the source). Write in third person (no "I" or "we," unless part of a quote), with plenty of facts and statistics to back up the information.

Reporters are trained to write in inverted pyramid style, where the first sentence, or lead, summarizes the story, and all subsequent details taper from most to least important (for more information, see the chart). Your press release should follow the same structure. The main principle behind the inverted pyramid style is so people can get the main idea of the story in the first paragraph, then choose whether or not they want to know more. When they've read enough, they'll move on. (Hmmm ... sounds a lot like interactions in the booth, doesn't it?)

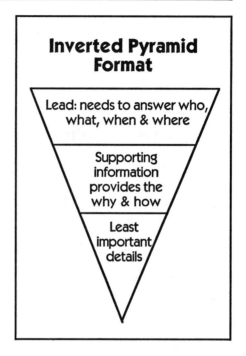

Inverted Pyramid Format

Lead: needs to answer who, what, when & where

Supporting information provides the why & how

Least important details

Keep in mind, editors may only use one out of every 10 releases they receive. If yours is well-written, it automatically has a better chance than those that aren't. Always include contact information at the top of the release. Provide phone number, pager or cell number, and e-mail address to make it easier for the reporter to get answers to any additional questions. Include the show name and your booth number.

What should you write about? Ask yourself what the readers or viewers most want to know, and then answer those questions. Don't get too technical, even when you're sending the release to a trade journal. Incorporate recent trends or statistics to create timeliness. Promote an interesting angle or unique product that will solve a common problem. You're never too small to attract the attention of the media if you have something interesting to say. But remember – stay focused on just one topic.

Possible topics for pre-show releases (also see the sample releases at the end of this chapter):

- Launch of a new product
- Promote celebrity guest in booth
- Report results of industry survey or research
- Dispute previously held stereotypes
- Announce a contest or award
- Tie in with current trend or news event

Become a resource for the media! You'll get even better results when you've built a relationship with the editor or reporter. Send them releases regularly, not just before a show. Also, let them know of other sources they might want to contact for the story.

Structure of a Press Release

• Print the words "FOR IMMEDIATE RELEASE" in the top left corner (or "FOR RELEASE ON ..." and insert a specific date), followed by your contact information: name, title, phone number and e-mail address, along with show name and booth number

• Start the body of the release with a dateline (such as "CHICAGO – June 1, 2001")

• Create a dynamic, attention-grabbing headline and center it in bold type (but don't get too "cute")

• Compose short sentences, with a maximum of 4 or 5 sentences per paragraph

• Leave a blank line between paragraphs and use 1-inch margins

• Use lines 50 to 60 characters long and avoid hyphens at the end of lines

• Write in active voice; avoid adjectives and adverbs and don't over-embellish or exaggerate

• Keep it to one page, but if it must be two pages, end page one with a complete paragraph (and center the word "More" at the bottom of page)

• Include contact info and subject at the top of page two

• End the release with "###" or "–30–" centered on the page

• Always check for spelling and accuracy; do days and dates agree?

You might also want to include any relevant photos with your release (but not if you're e-mailing — reporters won't open attachments), along with some basic background on your company. You may even want to create a complete press kit for distribution prior to or in the Press Room at the show (for more information about the press room, see Chapter 13: More Than Selling Real Estate).

Creating Press Kits

Creating E-mail Press Releases

•• Make your headline the subject line; or you may precede it with the words, "FOR IMMEDIATE RELEASE:"

•• Keep your lead paragraph to 40 words or less

•• Write a 30-second story (sound bite) with a maximum 200 words (4 to 5 paragraphs)

•• Include contact information at the bottom

A successful press kit should include:
• Photos (typically 5-by-7-inch or 8-by-10-inch photos, or transparencies in sleeves with captions and contact info on labels; could also be on CD)
• Brochures, fliers and other collateral material
• Corporate background information (one page, "at-a-glance" style)
• Any related press releases that are new and relevant to the show
• List of satisfied clients who are willing to be contacted
• Roster of company spokespeople who will be available for interviews at the show

Put all the information in a glossy color pocket folder (which can be custom-printed, or simply a standard folder with your company label on the front). Include a printed label on the cover that mentions the show name, your booth number, and the news peg. Make the kit tactile by including product samples, if possible. You could also include some kind of promotional item, but be careful! A reputable journalist will not accept any kind of gift that appears to be an attempt to influence their story.

Never ask to review a story before it goes to print!

Following Up

Resist the urge to call to make sure they received your release. If you do decide to call, make sure

---

 Tips for Working with TV Reporters

•◆ Create a very brief release (or simply create an outline); read it out loud before sending
•◆ Spell out any difficult words phonetically
•◆ Send out materials with at least a three-week lead time
•◆ Consider creating a 90-second video news release (VNR) in broadcast-quality format – but be careful not to sound like a commercial! (If your narration is recorded on a separate track, the clips can also be used as "b-roll", or supplemental footage.)
•◆ Before being interviewed, make a mental list of the points you want to cover or that may come up; practice speaking to avoid any unpleasant speech patterns (such as hissing "s" or a monotone)
•◆ Use plain English and speak in sound bites (10-20 second answers); speak slowly, pausing briefly between sentences
•◆ In your interview, give lots of tips and quick facts; don't try too hard to plug your company or product
•◆ Wear solid colors in mid- to dark tones (small patterns can cause a dizziness on camera); avoid pure white, black or red clothing, as well as any shiny jewelry
•◆ Assume all microphones are live until you're told you're off the air; look at the interviewer, not the camera, unless you're told otherwise, and keep your gestures small
•◆ Be casually enthusiastic and remember to SMILE!

you have a solid reason to do so, such as additional information that's just become available, and then ask if they have time to talk. Reporters who are genuinely interested in your story will call or e-mail you for more information. When they do, be prepared to respond quickly! Remember, they are often working on very strict deadlines and can't wait on you.

Schmooze 'Em or Lose 'Em?

Press Releases that Stand Out

Instead of a press release, send them a teaser to create anticipation!

For example, create fortune cookies with a question about your company or product, along with your booth number for the answer. Distribute these prior to the show or in the press room.

Before you go all-out to plan a media event or press conference at your next show, ask yourself how you plan to stand out. Staging a ribbon-cutting in your booth as a photo opportunity won't cut it. Unless you're making a major announcement or unveiling a new product, there may be a better way to get the attention of the press. (Most editors prefer to gather news one-on-one anyway.) Good alternatives include scheduling personal interviews or product demonstrations, or inviting the press to your customer hospitality event (more on hosting one of these in Chapter 14: Housewarmings).

But if you are introducing a new product that will have significant impact (both inside and outside your industry), or if you need to reach a maximum number of reporters in a short amount of time, a press conference may be your best solution. Work with Show Management several weeks or months in advance to schedule your press conference (early in the day is best) and avoid competing with other exhibitors. Send formal, written invitations to the media prior to the show (no e-mail or faxes).

Virtual Press Rooms

Create a press room on your corporate Web site or consider creating a CD-ROM press kit.

A good Web press room should include:

- Name, phone and e-mail information for primary media contacts in your company

- Trade show calendar with links to relevant releases

- E-mail link for scheduling interviews at the show

Make it worth their time! At the event, hand out your press kits as the reporters arrive (include a copy of the speaker's statements), and always start on time. Keep the event short and simple (20 minutes or less), with plenty of visuals to support your message (charts, graphs, video, photos, or props). Follow with a question-and-answer session. Have staffers available afterwards to schedule in-depth interviews. Anticipate the kinds of questions you're likely to receive. Practice how to answer rude, cynical or hostile questions with grace and poise. Don't volunteer any additional information or opinions.

After the event, follow up to thank the reporters who attended and answer any additional questions. For key media people who couldn't attend, give them a one-page summary of what was said, along with copies of any appropriate visuals.

Congratulations! You're News!

There it is – a two-page article in the hot industry magazine, featuring your new product! Once you stop dancing around the office, what should you do?

First, send a thank-you note to the reporter. Let him or her know you appreciate the well-written story and report any responses you've received. But never send a gift! Be gracious. Even if the coverage was not all you'd hoped for, it was free, remember?

Keep a journal of all the coverage you receive, along with clippings (or tapes of any broadcast coverage). Don't ask the reporters to send you clips (some will send them anyway as a courtesy), but you can ask them to alert you when a story will appear. Even if you don't appear in the next issue following the show, don't count that publication out. Keep building that relationship with the reporter or editor; you never know

Creating a Winning Media Event

When Nissan wanted to introduce their Xterra SUV at the North American International Auto Show, they decided to drive it out of a giant blue backpack! But first, they sent postcard invitations to members of the press. The front of the postcard had a photo of a giant zipper.

When reporters arrived at the event, they received media kits in regular-sized backpacks, just like the one on stage, bearing the Nissan logo. Then, with video, music and fanfare, the backpack began to "squirm." Soon, the vehicle appeared out of the 25-foot tall backpack, symbolizing how the Xterra was a "backpack on wheels."

Why go to such extremes? At the NAIA Show, there are typically more than 50 press conferences. "We have to do something to stand out," says Nissan's Bill Garlin. So they turned to the George P. Johnson Company to design the backpack event.

Was it worth it? Although they don't have exact numbers of how much media coverage they received, Garlin says the response was "massive and positive." And he's still seeing those backpacks more than two years later! But this kind of exposure doesn't come cheap. A splashy media event can run several hundred thousand dollars.

when they will have an assignment that your company fits into perfectly!

The results of good media coverage go way beyond a measurement of column inches or airtime. Look at the overall impact of the stories and the response generated. Sometimes one powerful new client can come from a simple two-inch sidebar in a major industry publication.

Toot your own horn! If you win any awards at the show, send out another press release, along with photos.

Resources

Gale Group
800-877-4253
www.galegroup.com

George P. Johnson Co.
310-965-4300
www.gpjco.com

Fictional Case Study: DigiCrayon

Scenario:
A small educational software company who wants to showcase their newest creation: a landscape design program, featuring an online gardening guide

Show:
Local Home & Garden Show, estimated 20,000 attendees over three days (28 hours); a horizontal consumer show

Exhibit:
10' x 10' booth

Goals:
Out of those who stop at the booth:
- Sell 250 software packages ($49.95 retail at a show special of $35; $8,750 total sales)
- Gather mailing list of 500 names
- Gain local media coverage (at least 2 stories)

Breakdown:
18 leads and 9 sales per hour

Budget:
$1,000	Space rental
$ 750	Booth design
$ 800	Show services
$ 750	Promotions
$ 400	Staffing
$ 300	Misc. expenses
$4,000	

Theme:
"Where Technology Blooms"

Booth Design:
- Use existing backwall graphic of a flower garden; blend potted plants (with "blooming" CDs) and a tree (with CD "fruit" hanging on it into the backwall
- Place an old computer monitor in the center of the backwall with plants growing out of it
- Include two stations (2' x 2' counters): one for demos and the other for lead management (with storage underneath
- Create an experience with sounds of birds, insects and water
- Add scents of flowers and rain

Staff:
- Two staffers in booth at all times, one at each station

Attire:
- Khaki pants with floral or Hawaiian shirts

Opening Lines:
- "What kind of garden does your computer grow?"
- "When was the last time your computer looked like this?" (referring to the display)

Qualifying:
- Find out if prospects own a home, plan to do any landscaping, and have a computer at home

Pre-Show Promotions:
- Send series of postcard mailers
  - Mail to prospects and garden club list
  - Front of card has a photo of a computer monitor with a plant growing out of it (like what will be in display) and the message, "Discover the hidden garden inside your computer."
  - Back of card mentions show special (when they bring the card to the booth)
- Partner with local greenhouse to promote and provide plants for the display in exchange for signage and mention in promotions
- Place fliers at partner greenhouse and in local libraries

Attractions:
- Software demo (hands-on) as well as virtual-to-real photo transitions on screen

Giveaways:
- Printout of an attendee's basic design (allowing only 2 to 3 minutes each so they can't do a complete design)

- CD jewel case with flower-shaped CD demo (very
  limited; include virtual-to-real photos), promotional
  catalog of other software
- A seed packet (provided by the partner greenhouse)

Media Relations:
- Send press releases to local newspapers, garden
  magazines, and TV stations

(See press release sample on next page.)

FOR IMMEDIATE RELEASE
Contact: Amy Smith   555-1234
         amy@anywhere.com
         Home & Garden Expo Booth #125

LOCAL SOFTWARE COMPANY PUTS GARDEN INSIDE COMPUTER

ANYWHERE, USA – April 1, 2001: If you've ever wanted to see how your garden will look before you plant it, stop by the Home & Garden Expo at the Convention Center April 27 to 29 and take a look.

DigiCrayon, creators of educational software titles, will be introducing their new landscaping program at the Expo. The program uses CAD technology to "map out" an unlimited number of planting possibilities. Then with a touch of computerized magic, the seasons change, showing the colors of both spring and fall over a period of several years.

"A common question beginning landscapers always ask is how the look of their yard will change over time," according to DigiCrayon's creative director Al Johnson. "Now they can use the computer to 'age' their designs."

In addition to the computer-aging techniques, garden enthusiasts can also look up plant information on the CD, including diagnosing basic problems.

###

Fictional Case Study: Purple Carrot Press

Scenario:
A children's book publisher wants to showcase their new line of collateral materials (stuffed toys, games, puzzles); two main characters to feature: Sunny the Frog and Alyssa

Show:
Regional book and toy retailers' show with an estimated 7,000 attendees over two days (14 hours); a vertical trade show

Exhibit:
20' x 30' island booth

Goals:
Out of those who stop at the booth:
- Gain 550 leads (stores to possibly carry products)
- Sign up 100 new retailers within 30 days of show
- Gain media coverage (at least one TV and one print)

Breakdown:
40 leads per hour

Budget:

$10,000	Space rental
$ 7,500	Booth design & new graphics
$8,000	Show services
$5,000	Shipping
$6,500	Travel & lodging (10 staffers)
$8,000	Promotions
$2,500	Staffing
$2,500	Misc. expenses
$50,000	

Theme:
"More than Just a Story"

Booth Design:
- Use existing island display frame with new graphics (oversized reproductions of actual storybook pages)
- Four product display stations (with a mix of books and other items; connected to giant book with arches); each has storage underneath
- Incorporate giant puzzles on floor
- Create an experience with sounds of frogs and insects, or books on tape being played over product stations (using plexiglass sound domes)
- Add scents of grass for Sunny the Frog and tea party items (cookies, lemonade) for Alyssa

Staff:
- At least eight staffers in booth at all times, one at each product station and one at each "page" of the giant book

Attire:
- Men wear green shirts and black pants (to blend with Sunny's stories); Women wear rose shirts and black skirts (to blend with Alyssa's stories)

Opening Lines:
- "When was the last time you played a game?"
- "Who's your favorite frog?" (Sunny, of course!)
- "How do you bring a book to life?"

Qualifying:
- Find out the prospect's type and size of store, target demographics, and who is in charge of buying decisions

Pre-Show Promotions:
- Send a series of mailers to clients and prospects
  - Mailer one: Postcard of Sunny the Frog
  - Mailer two: Postcard of Alyssa

- Mailer three: 3-D pop-up "book" with a card invitation inside (with instructions to bring the completed card to the booth; also to save the pop-up for a surprise to come later)

Attractions:
- Costumed characters of Sunny the Frog and Alyssa on hand in the booth (alternating 20 minutes on and off) to pose for photos with attendees in front of the giant book
- One product station demonstrating the new Sunny game, with attendees encouraged to participate
- Special offer: Opportunity to host costume character in the client's store with a $1,000 wholesale order placed within 30 days of the show

Giveaways:
- Photos (fit in pre-show mailer pop-up book as frame)
- Drawing for $500 of bonus merchandise (using pre-show lead cards)

Media Relations:
Send press releases and photos to trade magazines and local TV stations; also take the characters to a local children's hospital the day before the show opens (See press release sample on next page.)

FOR IMMEDIATE RELEASE
Contact: Pete Davis   555-4444
pete@purplecarrot.com
Book & Toy Show Booth #820

CHARACTERS TO VISIT CHILDREN'S HOSPITAL

CHICAGO, IL – June 28, 2001: Patients at Children's Hospital will get a visit from two of their favorite characters on July 17.

Sunny the Frog and Alyssa will be making an appearance the day before the Regional Book & Toy Show opens at Navy Pier. Purple Carrot Press, creators of Sunny and Alyssa, recently hired a costume design company to bring their two most popular characters to life.

"Kids of all ages love Sunny and Alyssa," says Dave Kimson, marketing manager for Purple Carrot. "We want to help brighten the day for some kids that need some extra-special love and attention."

At the Book & Toy Show, Purple Carrot Press will be introducing some new products for both Sunny and Alyssa. The characters will also be attending the show, posing for photos with attendees in the Purple Carrot booth.

###

Putting the
Roof On

Once you've built your house and designed a fantastic interior, would you skip putting a roof on? No way! Besides being irresponsible, you'd be letting all your hard work and planning go to waste.

It's the same with your trade show leads. If you don't have a system in place to manage them, follow up, and measure your results, you might as well skip the exhibiting experience all together.

You're not finished with your exhibit until you've done some ...

Weatherproofing

If one of the major reasons to exhibit is to collect qualified leads, then why are 80 percent of
leads never followed up on? One reason is that
exhibitors don't have a plan in place for managing those leads before going to the show. Don't
assume the prospects will contact you!

The first step in any lead management plan
should be to design an effective lead card.

Lead Cards that Work

Exhibit managers and their marketing departments have very different perspectives on collecting leads, according to Ivan Lazarev of
bCard.net, developers of customized loyalty programs using smart cards. "The exhibit manager
needs a user-friendly tool to collect as many
leads as possible, and to pre-qualify them. The
marketing department wants to see sales conversion and branding via post-show surveys,"
Lazarev says. A good lead card can keep both
sides happy by gathering not only basic contact
information, but also some relevant demographics.

Begin by creating multiple-choice questions
with checkboxes to make the card quick and
easy to fill out (the customer should be able to
complete it in a 5- to 7-minute interaction). Use
qualifying questions (see Chapter 7: Finishing
Touches) developed by both the sales and marketing departments, including: demographics,
level of interest, products currently using, timing, budget, and buying authority. Aimee Firor
of ExpoExchange, an electronic lead manage-

> "The biggest
> problem is that
> a majority of
> exhibitors
> don't know
> what to do
> [to follow up],
> so they don't
> do anything."
>
> - Aimee Firor,
> ExpoExchange

Pre-Qualifying Saves Time

If you've chosen to do a pre-show mailer that requires them to fill out a card and bring it to the booth, you can quickly see if they're qualified.

Also, by incorporating a live presentation in the booth, you can pre-qualify several people at once. After the presentation, staffers only need to follow up at that moment with the hottest prospects. All other visitors are entered into the database of leads from their profile cards, which were filled out prior to the presentation.

ment provider, suggests asking your sales reps what three things they most need to know for more efficient follow-up.

Rank leads by some type of priority system (A, B or C; hot, warm or cold). This helps the sales force know who to follow up with first. Always ask prospects how they want you to follow up with them, and make note of that on the card. Leave room for staffers to include additional notes necessary to remind them about the customer's individual situation. Include a place for staffers to initial or sign the lead card, to give you a contact for any questions that arise. This also helps track who's been most successful at gathering leads (more on this in Chapter 16: Rewarding the Crew).

Ideally, the card should fit comfortably in your hand (postcard-size is good), and can also be bound into pads for easier use. Keep a stapler on hand to staple business cards or badge scanner printouts to the card. A word of caution here: don't blindly depend on the badge scanner. The data may be incomplete or incorrect. (Or worse yet, the system could go down.) Always verify the information on the scanner. Gathering accurate and complete information is important because those staffing the booth are often not the ones following up!

Have a way to link your leads to your customer database, so the leads can be tracked over time. (Remember – a majority of leads gathered at a show may take anywhere from 6 to 36 months to become clients.) "People have to justify their ROI even more than before," says Firor. "So they need more efficient ways to follow up." If you develop an organized method for tracking the leads, you can more accurately justify your ROI for each show (more on that in Chapter 12: Seeing Return on Your Investment).

Computerized Lead Gathering

Moving into the 21st Century, there are a plethora of electronic lead gathering and lead management tools available. But just like with

> **Any lead not followed up within 30 days is dead!**

 Making the Most of Lead Cards

- ➡ Chicago Exhibit Productions designed a lead card that looked like an airline ticket, since they were giving away a weekend trip for two. To enter the drawing, visitors brought their card to the booth, already filled out with contact information and answers to questions such as: buying influence, exhibit size and how many shows, and annual budget.

- ➡ Wood Associates reinforced their "All-American" theme with a lead card that looked like a ballot. Staffers asked visitors what products they were interested in and when their next event was coming up.

- ➡ EliteXPO created a card that asked the visitor's job title, whether or not they were the final decision maker, who they were currently using, and what they look for in a shipping provider.

the good old paper lead cards, you have to have a system that will work.

If you're simply scanning badges and calling those slips of paper your leads, you're in for a big disappointment. The problem with many computerized lead gathering methods is that they're basically an electronic phone book, with just names and addresses, according to Penny Ripple of RippleWare, a lead management software company. Instead, electronic lead cards should mirror paper ones, complete with basic demographics and qualifying information, such as budget and buying timeline.

> There's a big difference between generating leads and managing them!

Incomplete lead gathering puzzles Ripple. "Companies are willing to spend millions of dollars a year (to attend shows) and yet they continue to be content to come home with business cards?" she asks. Worse yet, since many people don't know what to do with all those cards, they just get trashed!

By asking the right qualifying questions, you will not only get the information your sales force needs to follow up, but you'll also know when to disengage as attendees "unqualify" themselves. For example, Ripple suggests that you find out the basics: are they ready (timing), willing (interested), and able (budget). If not, let them go!

The biggest benefit to computerized lead management comes after the show, when you are able to sort the data. For example, with RippleWare, you can generate reports based on geographic location, company size, or any of your other lead card categories, complete with charts and graphs. By doing this, you can see that a majority of your leads came from small companies in the Southeast, not from the larger West Coast companies you had targeted. Use that data to discover what worked and what didn't. (More on this in Chapter 12: Seeing Return on Your Investment.)

Another benefit of computerized leads, says Lazarev, is to have a link between your customer database and the data collected at the show. Then you can track the leads over time to see your results. Some other benefits of electronic lead management:
- Makes following up easier
- Activates immediately; can auto-send a thank-you minutes after their visit to your booth
- Stamps with date and time to help you determine when the booth is busiest
- Helps analyze how well you attracted your target audience

Before investing in lead gathering or management software, be sure to ask if the program can be customized, as well as what kinds of badges it reads. Find out if it will work with your existing customer database program. Also, it doesn't hurt to check out the company's tech support (a crucial component in a crisis) and ask to speak with some current clients.

Even if you've done an outstanding job of gathering leads with whatever system you choose, you won't see any results unless you do systematic, timely follow-up.

The 48/10/30 Plan

- First contact: within 48 hours (24 hours for hottest prospects)
- Second, more extensive contact: within 10 days of meeting (5 for hot ones)
- Third contact: call to follow up on packet within 30 days of meeting (then continue following up about every six weeks)

> **Always keep a backup copy of your electronic leads – and never, ever pack your leads in your exhibit case!**

With every day that goes by, your leads are getting colder. To keep them hot (and to keep from letting your competitors get to those prospects ahead of you), make that first contact right away. Your hottest leads need to be followed up each day of the show – don't wait until you get back to the office. And all leads should have their first contact from you within 48 hours after visiting your booth.

Now, this doesn't have to be complicated. A simple thank-you e-mail that reiterates what follow-up action they can expect is a very good method to use. It simply gets your company

---

 ## More Follow-Up Ideas

➡ Offer a "fax-on-demand" service in your booth – let people fax the information they need back to their office

➡ Create a customized brochure that can be emailed to the prospect as a PDF (Portable Document Format: a "What you see is what you get" file); make sure they will be expecting it, so they will open the attachment

➡ Create an online newsletter to keep in regular contact with your leads

➡ Announce the winners of your in-booth contest by posting the names on your web site, then send an e-mail to all your leads telling them to log on and find out if they won

➡ Send your pre-show mailers for other shows throughout the year that the prospect or customer might want to attend

➡ Use incentive programs to encourage attendees to fill out post-show surveys

name in front of them again and confirms that you (or someone else from your company) will be following up.

Some will argue that you should send a complete information kit via FedEx, so it's waiting for them back at the office. The problem with that? There are millions of other things waiting for their attention too! It's much better to time your mailing to arrive two or three days after the prospect has returned, in order to get their full attention.

The best way to accomplish this is to designate a lead manager to coordinate each day's leads and forward the hottest ones back to the office to begin immediate follow-up. Or, you may

Keep in mind, vertical shows will have a much higher ratio of qualified leads.

 Personalizing Follow-Up Mailings

You've heard the importance of personalizing a form letter. Sweepstakes companies are famous for it – sprinkling the recipient's name throughout the letter to make them think it was written just for them. But true personalization goes far beyond that!

Use the information you gathered on your lead card, such as where they are located or what their most important needs are. Incorporate items like, "When Client XYZ was facing [the same problem the attendee indicated], we helped them find a way to …."

Why is this effective? The prospect is much more likely to keep that mailing handy, instead of letting it hit the trash like so many others received. So next time you want to personalize a form letter, don't use flat methods of name-dropping like, "Would you like to save $250 a year, Joe?" Liven it up with some creative touches. You'll get a lot more attention!

"Bad Follow-Up is Worse than None at All" (from TradeShowTips Online, Issues #3 & #11)

Longing for a way to stand out from your competition? It may sound too simple to be true, but prompt and thorough follow-up may be one of the best ways to stand out from the crowd.

Here are some examples of what NOT to do:

•• After visiting a travel booth at a local show, I received information in a timely manner, but what did I receive? The letter was addressed to someone else, congratulating her on an upcoming honeymoon in Bermuda (I was planning a vacation in Las Vegas!), but the travel brochures they sent were all for Vegas. Needless to say, I never called them. If they can't even stuff an envelope, would I trust them with my travel plans? Definitely not!

•• At one booth, I specifically asked to be contacted in a couple of months. They followed up with a phone call the Monday following the show, then later that week with an e-mail and an information packet, complete with a contract! Another phone call and e-mail came within two weeks. Was my name the only one they got from that show? It certainly felt like it!

•• One exhibitor left a voicemail message saying, "I've been trying to do all these calls and get them out of the way ..."

•• After another show, I received a follow-up e-mail thanking me for my "recent interest." Nothing wrong with that, right? The problem was that the e-mail was sent in August regarding a show held the previous November! (And you thought e-mail was fast!)

•• When one exhibitor I was especially interested in didn't send anything, I actually called them several weeks after the show to remind them I was looking forward to receiving their materials. They never did respond!

•• Probably the most remarkable "don't" came from a company thanking me for stopping by their booth at a show I never even attended!

want to consider hiring a fulfillment house to help with lead
management. They can assist
with everything from telemarketing to literature and sample fulfillment.

Keith   Milburn,   owner   of
Innovative Fulfillment Solutions,
says when working with a fulfillment house, you should have all
of your materials to them at least
four weeks prior to the show (to
allow time to set up your account,
input any SKU numbers, and create custom letters). You also need
to identify which items should be
sent to each lead (this can be
accomplished by checking boxes
on your lead card).

Ways to Follow Up

- Phone calls
- Personal appointments
- Product literature or catalogs
- Thank-you note or letter
- Product samples
- E-mail

Customizing cover letters doesn't mean simply
changing the name and address on each one.
Instead, they can be personalized according to
the type of needs or product interest. The
accompanying packet of literature can be customized as well. For example, your hot leads
might receive an extensive information packet
and cover letter, while warm leads receive a couple of basic brochures and a letter. You can also
assemble an individualized collection of samples
for each person who requests them at the show.

A fulfillment house will provide warehouse
space, computerized lead tracking, and the labor
to stuff packets. In return, you can expect to pay
administration   fees   (for   managing   your
account), storage fees (per pallet or square foot),
and per-kit assembly fees (which can range from
$2 to $5 each for a basic packet or sample kit).
If you think these costs seem like too much, consider what you're spending in lost hours for one

E-mail Follow-Up Etiquette

•◆ Make your subject line get to the point; perhaps include show name so they know it's not junk mail

•◆ Never mass-mail without doing it as a blind carbon copy (or use the mail list feature) to avoid sending each person a long list of everyone else's address!

•◆ Watch your tone, especially if using humor or sarcasm

•◆ Never use ALL CAPS – it's perceived as shouting

•◆ Double- and triple-check spelling and grammar

•◆ Never include attachments – instead, direct prospects to your corporate Web site for more information

•◆ Think before you write, and especially before you hit "Send"!

of your own people to stuff all those envelopes!

Milburn says that another advantage of using a fulfillment house is that each contact with the prospect is tracked so you can see what really "sold" them on your company. And just in case your staff didn't do a good job of qualifying the leads at the show, you can outsource that too. Milburn's team will call leads to determine their level of interest, and sometimes prospects are more candid over the phone about their needs.

Did you know?

•◆ It takes an average of $1,117 and 3.7 contacts to close a field lead, but only $625 and 1.3 contacts to close a trade show lead (because you've built a relationship with the prospect). *(Source: CEIR Report #SM17)*
•◆ Over 50% of attendees maintain a file of material requested at trade shows. *(Source: CEIR Report #AC24C)*

The Secrets of Follow-Up

If pre-show mailers are the equivalent of invitations to a party, then following up is the same as sending thank-you notes to your guests. Terri Crim of Modern Postcard says that follow-up should be an automatic part of your marketing, just like pre-show mailers. Or, as Lori Marshall from Wood Associates puts it, "Every prospect is important ... they took the time [to stop by the booth], so why shouldn't I take the time to thank them?" Not surprisingly, Marshall's follow-up arrives in the form of a handwritten thank-you note.

Now, here are some easy keys to following up and standing out from the crowd.

1. Make your follow-up timely. (One exhibitor wondered why a prospect was being so evasive on the phone when she called to follow up. She later learned that her competitor was meeting with the prospect at the moment she called. Lesson learned: Be the first to follow up!)

2. Use the notes on your lead cards to personalize the follow-up. (The travel agency in the TradeShowTips example on page 178 at least had that part right; they just sent it to the wrong person!)

3. Reinforce your exhibit theme in your follow up to help with recall. (Bankers Advertising continued their food-themed booth by sending mailers that looked like recipe cards, along with a shopping list pad.)

4. Again, using your lead cards, make sure you know which show the prospect attended. Keep each show's leads separated, or use a color-coding system.

5. Always respond in the way the prospect told you to. Attendees are annoyed when they don't receive the information they were promised. This proves you weren't listening to their needs. If they want a catalog and you call them on the phone, they will just tell you again to please send a catalog. Get it right the first time!

> "Too many people get overwhelmed after the show and drop the ball, even though they have good intentions."
>
> - Aimee Firor, Expo Exchange

Hot prospects typically buy within 30 days. Warm ones (which are the majority) may take much longer. Make sales reps accountable for the leads and monitor their progress for at least six months. Keep following up until they "buy or die" – it can take several contacts to close a sale. Since most of your competitors will give up after one or two tries, you can win the sale by sheer persistence.

Remember ... your job doesn't end the minute the show is over. Instead, the most important part begins! You have those lead cards – now turn them into money in the bank!

 ## Vocabulary

Badge scanner: a device used to "read" the attendees' badges, contracted by show management; data can be saved electronically or printed out

Loyalty program: a system to track activity for individual attendees and reward them

Mag-stripe card: magnetized strip on the back of the card that contains data (similar to the strip on a credit card)

Smart card: similar to mag card, only it has an embedded micro chip

2-D bar code: printed on attendee badge; can be scanned to capture registration information

Resources

bCard.net
>   800-215-2266
>   www.bcard.net

ExpoExchange
>   800-448-1883
>   www.expoexchange.com

**Innovative Fulfillment
Solutions**
>   888-275-3000
>   www.ifssolutions.com

RippleWare
>   904-454-3140
>   www.rippleware.com

Modern Postcard
>   800-959-8365
>   www.modernpostcard.com

Fictional Case Study: DigiCrayon

Scenario:

A small educational software company who wants to showcase their newest creation: a landscape design program, featuring an online gardening guide

Show:

Local Home & Garden Show, estimated 20,000 attendees over three days (28 hours); a horizontal consumer show

Exhibit:
10' x 10' booth

Goals:
Out of those who stop at the booth:
- Sell 250 software packages ($49.95 retail at a show special of $35; $8,750 total sales)
- Gather mailing list of 500 names
- Gain local media coverage (at least 2 stories)

Breakdown:
18 leads and 9 sales per hour

Budget:

	$1,000	Space rental
	$ 750	Booth design
	$ 800	Show services
	$ 750	Promotions
	$ 400	Staffing
	$ 300	Misc. expenses
	$4,000	

Theme:
"Where Technology Blooms"

Booth Design:
- Use existing backwall graphic of a flower garden; blend potted plants (with "blooming" CDs) and a tree (with CD "fruit" hanging on it into the backwall
- Place an old computer monitor in the center of the backwall with plants growing out of it
- Include two stations (2' x 2' counters): one for demos and the other for lead management (with storage underneath
- Create an experience with sounds of birds, insects and water
- Add scents of flowers and rain

Staff:
- Two staffers in booth at all times, one at each station

Attire:
- Khaki pants with floral or Hawaiian shirts

Opening Lines:
- "What kind of garden does your computer grow?"
- "When was the last time your computer looked like this?" (referring to the display)

Qualifying:
- Find out if prospects own a home, plan to do any land-scaping, and have a computer at home

Pre-Show Promotions:
- Send series of postcard mailers
  - Mail to prospects and garden club list
  - Front of card has a photo of a computer monitor with a plant growing out of it (like what will be in display) and the message, "Discover the hidden garden inside your computer."
  - Back of card mentions show special (when they bring the card to the booth)
- Partner with local greenhouse to promote and pro-vide plants for the display in exchange for signage and mention in promotions
- Place fliers at partner greenhouse and in local libraries

Attractions:
- Software demo (hands-on) as well as virtual-to-real photo transitions on screen

Giveaways:
- Printout of an attendee's basic design (allowing only 2 to 3 minutes each so they can't do a complete design)

- CD jewel case with flower-shaped CD demo (very limited; include virtual-to-real photos), promotional catalog of other software
- A seed packet (provided by the partner greenhouse)

Media Relations:

- Send press releases to local newspapers, garden magazines, and TV stations

Follow-Up:

- For purchasers, send a thank-you e-mail ("48"), followed by a note on a floral card with a gift certificate to use at the partner greenhouse ("10"), and then call in 2 to 3 weeks to answer any technical questions ("30")
- For prospects, send a brochure with a special offer to receive a greenhouse gift certificate with the purchase of software

---

DigiCrayon Contact Information Form
Home & Garden Show 2001

Name _____ **Phone** _____
Address _____ **E-mail** _____
_____

Software interest: ❏ Landscaping   ❏ Educational   ❏ Other

Computer: ❏ Mac OS   ❏ Windows   **Home:** ❏ Own ❏ Rent

Follow-Up desired: ❏ Catalog   ❏ Phone call   ❏ Other
              ❏ Mailing list for new products

Comments:_____ **Staffer:** _____
_____ **Code:** A   B   C

Fictional Case Study: Purple Carrot Press

Scenario:

A children's book publisher wants to showcase their new line of collateral materials (stuffed toys, games, puzzles); two main characters to feature: Sunny the Frog and Alyssa

Show:

Regional book and toy retailers' show with an estimated 7,000 attendees over two days (14 hours); a vertical trade show

Exhibit:

20' x 30' island booth

Goals:

Out of those who stop at the booth:
- Gain 550 leads (stores to possibly carry products)
- Sign up 100 new retailers within 30 days of show
- Gain media coverage (at least one TV and one print)

Breakdown:

40 leads per hour

Budget:

$10,000	Space rental
$ 7,500	Booth design & new graphics
$8,000	Show services
$5,000	Shipping
$6,500	Travel & lodging (10 staffers)
$8,000	Promotions
$2,500	Staffing
$2,500	Misc. expenses
$50,000	

Theme:

"More than Just a Story"

Booth Design:
- Use existing island display frame with new graphics (oversized reproductions of actual storybook pages)
- Four product display stations (with a mix of books and other items; connected to giant book with arches); each has storage underneath
- Incorporate giant puzzles on floor
- Create an experience with sounds of frogs and insects, or books on tape being played over product stations (using plexiglass sound domes)
- Add scents of grass for Sunny the Frog and tea party items (cookies, lemonade) for Alyssa

Staff:
- At least eight staffers in booth at all times, one at each product station and one at each "page" of the giant book

Attire:
- Men wear green shirts and black pants (to blend with Sunny's stories); Women wear rose shirts and black skirts (to blend with Alyssa's stories)

Opening Lines:
- "When was the last time you played a game?"
- "Who's your favorite frog?" (Sunny, of course!)
- "How do you bring a book to life?"

Qualifying:
- Find out the prospect's type and size of store, target demographics, and who is in charge of buying decisions

Pre-Show Promotions:
- Send a series of mailers to clients and prospects
  - Mailer one: Postcard of Sunny the Frog
  - Mailer two: Postcard of Alyssa

- Mailer three: 3-D pop-up "book" with a card invitation inside (with instructions to bring the completed card to the booth; also to save the pop--
up for a surprise to come later)

Attractions:
- Costumed characters of Sunny the Frog and Alyssa
on hand in the booth (alternating 20 minutes on and
off) to pose for photos with attendees in front of
the giant book
- One product station demonstrating the new Sunny
game, with attendees encouraged to participate
- Special offer: Opportunity to host costume character in the client's store with a $1,000 wholesale
order placed within 30 days of the show

Giveaways:
- Photos (fit in pre-show mailer pop-up book as frame)
- Drawing for $500 of bonus merchandise (using pre-
show lead cards)

Media Relations:
Send press releases to trade magazines and local TV
stations; also take the characters to a local children's
hospital the day before the show opens

Follow-Up:
- For all leads, send an e-mail thank-you and announce
the winner of the $500 of free products ("48")
- For hot prospects, personally call them within a week
to finalize their order; for warm leads, send them a
catalog or brochure ("10")
- For new clients, send a welcome letter "signed" by
Alyssa and Sunny: "We're looking forward to playing
with your young customers!" ("30")
- Send a post-show survey via e-mail or fax to all
leads about 4 to 6 weeks after the show

Purple Carrot Press Contact Information
Regional Book & Toy Show – July 2001

Company Name _____   Contact _____

Address _____   Title _____

_____   Phone _____

Web _____   Fax _____

E-mail _____   Current Client? Y N

Interested in: ❑ Sunny ❑ Alyssa ❑ Other: _____
❑ Books ❑ Dolls ❑ Dolls ❑ Games

Urgency: ❑ Immediate ❑ 6-12 months ❑ Future

Store volume: ❑ <$500 K ❑ $500 K-1 M ❑ $1-3 M ❑ $3 M+

Age range of customers: ❑ 0-2 ❑ 2-4 ❑ 4-6 ❑ 6+

Store type: ❑ Book ❑ Toy ❑ Education ❑ Other

Follow Up: ❑ Catalog ❑ Phone call ❑ Sales rep ❑ Other

Buying Influence: ❑ Recommend ❑ Approve ❑ Buy

Comments: _____

_____   **Staffer** _____

Seeing Return on Your Investment

Did you know?

•◦ Companies spend an estimated $51 billion per year on conventions and trade shows. (*Source: Convention Industry Council*)
•◦ 61% of exhibitors don't do any kind of ROI measurements. (*Source: 2001 reader survey by EXHIBITOR Magazine, Rochester, Minn.*)

How do you measure success? That all depends on what your goals are for the show. Remember how you were supposed to set quantifiable, measurable goals (from Chapter 1)? By using those numbers, you can evaluate how close your results came to meeting or exceeding them.

What are some aspects you can measure?
- Total number of leads gathered
- Attendance at booth
- Number of entry forms or pre-show vouchers turned in at the booth
- Sales at the show
- Amount of promotional items or samples given away
- Visitor response to your booth
- Press coverage received
- Costs per visitor or per lead
- Follow-up and post-show sales

What methods or tools can you use to measure results?
- Lead cards
- In-booth surveys
- Post-show surveys

> You should always evaluate your results before automatically signing up to exhibit next year.

- Sales tracking
- Media clips

Understand that a sale can rarely be attributed entirely to one exhibit. There are an infinite number of factors, such as ads, salesperson rapport, and recommendations from peers that can factor into the final decision. (That's why exhibits should be a part of your integrated marketing plan.) Because of this, you should evaluate both your return on investment (ROI) and objectives (ROO).

Calculating ROI

Counting sales or leads is only one tool to measure ROI. Listed below are some other quick and easy formulas to use to determine your success. Don't just calculate your results for one show. Instead, use these formulas to keep track of all of your shows from year to year. It's only by comparing results that you can ultimately discover how successful you've been.

For these examples, the total number of leads generated was 150, with a total exhibiting cost of $15,000. Sales that resulted from the show were $28,000.

Percent of goal achieved: Actual numbers (leads, sales, etc.) divided by your Goal

Example:	Leads gathered	150
	Divided by goal	÷ 125
	Percent of goal	120%

Cost per qualified lead: Amount invested to exhibit divided by the total number of qualified leads

Example:	Amount invested	$15,000
	# of qualified leads	÷ 150
	Cost/qualified lead	$100

Send thank-you notes to each booth staffer and report results. Keep them posted on any big sales that result from one of their leads.

Cost per impression: Amount invested to exhibit divided by the total number of booth visitors (This number can be calculated by counting the number of people who attended a presentation, registered for a contest, etc., which may actually be higher than your estimate.)

    Example: Amount invested $15,000
              # of visitors   ÷ 700
              Cost per impression $21.43

Percent of leads converted to sales:
Number of sales divided by the total number of leads generated

    Example: Number of sales   25
              # of leads   ÷ 150
              % of leads to sales   16.7%

Percent of total attendees attracted:
Total number of qualified leads divided by the total show attendees

    Example: Number of leads   150
              # of attendees   ÷5,000
              % of attendees attracted   3%

Sales made per dollar spent: Total amount of sales (in a given time frame) divided by the amount invested to exhibit (can also be calculated from projected sales)

    Example: Amount of sales $28,000
              Amount invested   ÷ 15,000
              Sales per dollar spent $1.87

Media impressions: Circulation of publication multiplied by 2.5 (the average <u>pass-along factor</u>); for broadcast, use Nielson or Arbitron ratings

    Example: Circulation   5,000
              Pass-along factor   x   2.5
              Media impressions   12,500

While sales objectives are typically bottom-line based, like the number of sales or leads, market-

> "You can't rest on your laurels. Nothing wilts faster than a laurel rested upon."
>
> -Mary Kay Ash, Founder, Mary Kay Cosmetics

ing objectives may not be so concrete. These often include promoting company awareness, generating press coverage, or doing market research. Instead of simple black-and-white formulas, you may need to resort to other methods to measure your success in these areas.

"You can't work in a vacuum! Educate your team as to what they need to do to make the process work ... Like an orchestra, you've got to play with all the parts in mind. When the trumpet stops, the saxophone picks up. If they didn't work together, it wouldn't be music, it would be cacophony."

– Penny Ripple, RippleWare

Using Surveys to Determine Your Return on Objectives

Perhaps as important as calculating your ROI is determining the return on your objectives. In order to better analyze your success, survey your booth visitors. Measure such things as audience awareness, brand-building, and staff effectiveness. Design clearly-worded questions and make them open-ended or use a ranking system. Offer incentives to visitors for taking the time to fill out the survey (which should be short).

Some surveys can be conducted as visitors exit the booth. Questions to ask include:
- What brought you to the exhibit (advertising, personal invitation, recommendation, company reputation, or just walking by)?
- Did the pre-show promotion have any influence on you stopping at the booth?
- How were you treated by the staff (were they knowledgeable and polite)?
- What was your response to any demonstrations or presentations?
- Has your impression of the company changed after visiting the exhibit?
- Did your decision to buy increase, decrease or remain about the same after visiting the booth?

Other questions should be asked several weeks following the show via e-mail or fax-back surveys, such as:

- What can you recall about our company or products?
- Did you receive adequate and timely follow up?
- Were your objectives met?

Other Aspects to Evaluate

Before you close the book on a show, you should also evaluate some things that aren't quite as measurable. For example, were all the deadlines met? If not, how can you improve your timing for the next show? Perhaps you need an electronic calendar that will alert you to approach-

Measuring Results

	Using Quantifiable Measurement Tools	Using Surveys or Other Methods
Leads	Total leads gathered or number of highly qualified leads; percent of target audience reached	Relate your totals to the show's overall audience trends (both size and quality) and the amount of promotions
Image	Percent of increase in purchases	Increased level of recall or name recognition; exhibit memorability
Presentations	Count the number in the audience	Ask for their response to the presentation, what they learned, and whether or not it influenced their decision
Media Coverage	Number of interviews or articles/broadcast stories that appear	Response to media coverage (track inquiries)

ing deadlines, such as the software program TRAQ-IT (see the Resource Guide).

What about your budget? Did you stay on target or go hideously overboard? Go over all your expenses and decide what areas can be reduced. If you found some things didn't work well, such as your pre-show promotions, determine if it was due to a lack of funds and then find ways to allocate the money in different places.

> "The road to success is always under construction."
>
> – Anonymous

Speaking of promotions, were your pre-show efforts successful at generating traffic? Did attendees seem to remember receiving your mailings? Were those who came more highly qualified? Teach staffers to ask attendees if they received the pre-show mailer, or better yet, provide a reason for attendees to bring their pre-show mailer to the booth (preferably filled out with their information). If a visitor doesn't remember receiving the pre-show promotion, ask them what influenced them to stop. Also decide if your in-booth attractions worked to streamline lead gathering.

Did attendees respond positively to your exhibit design? Was it functional and of adequate size to accomplish your goals? Perhaps you need to increase your booth size next year if you had the good fortune of a very crowded booth. Analyze if your graphics worked to draw people in and pre-qualify them. Were people confused about what you do?

What about your staff? Did you have an adequate number in the booth to handle your traffic? Were they the right people to interact with visitors? Perhaps you can correct some problems with more in-depth training before your next show. Maybe you already have a great staff, but they just need some motivation (see more on this in Chapter 16: Rewarding the Crew).

Now, how about your lead gathering? Did your chosen method work well? Were the leads managed properly and followed up on quickly? Perhaps you can implement a tracking system to better indicate when a trade show lead becomes a client, which will give you a truer picture of your ROI.

Getting Feedback from Staffers

One of the most often overlooked ways to determine if your exhibit performed well is to simply ask the people who worked the booth. Design an evaluation form for staffers to fill out within a week after the show. Like the attendee surveys, make it brief and use checkboxes. Questions to ask include:

- How productive were the booth's logistics (location, size, traffic flow)?
- Were the marketing methods effective (pre-show promotions, booth attractions, giveaways)?
- Which products generated the most interest? What should be included next time?
- Was staffing effective (number of staff, appropriateness of scheduling, adequacy of training)?
- Were there too many or not enough exhibit supplies (order forms, lead cards and other literature)?
- How was traffic in the booth (both quality and quantity)?
- How efficiently did you gather leads (both quality and quantity; also the lead-gathering process)?
- What were your overall impressions of the show (including a comparison of our booth to others at the show)?

Have a post-show meeting with everyone who staffed the booth to find out what response they received to the exhibit and also what information they gathered about competitors or the industry in general.

Resources

TRAQ-IT
888-869-4677
www.traqit.com

Vocabulary

Pass-along factor: the average number of people who see a single copy of any one issue of a publication

Fictional Case Study: DigiCrayon

Scenario:
A small educational software company who wants to showcase their newest creation: a landscape design program, featuring an online gardening guide

Show:
Local Home & Garden Show, estimated 20,000 attendees over three days (28 hours); a horizontal consumer show

Exhibit:
10' x 10' booth

Goals:
Out of those who stop at the booth:
- Sell 250 software packages ($49.95 retail at a show special of $35; $8,750 total sales)
- Gather mailing list of 500 names
- Gain local media coverage (at least 2 stories)

Breakdown:
18 leads and 9 sales per hour

Budget:
$1,000	Space rental
$ 750	Booth design
$ 800	Show services
$ 750	Promotions
$ 400	Staffing
$ 300	Misc. expenses
$4,000	

Theme:
"Where Technology Blooms"

Booth Design:
- Use existing backwall graphic of a flower garden; blend potted plants (with "blooming" CDs) and a tree (with CD "fruit" hanging on it into the backwall
- Place an old computer monitor in the center of the backwall with plants growing out of it
- Include two stations (2' x 2' counters): one for demos and the other for lead management (with storage underneath
- Create an experience with sounds of birds, insects and water
- Add scents of flowers and rain

Staff:
- Two staffers in booth at all times, one at each station

Attire:
- Khaki pants with floral or Hawaiian shirts

Opening Lines:
- "What kind of garden does your computer grow?"
- "When was the last time your computer looked like this?" (referring to the display)

Qualifying:
- Find out if prospects own a home, plan to do any landscaping, and have a computer at home

Pre-Show Promotions:
- Send series of postcard mailers
  - Mail to prospects and garden club list
  - Front of card has a photo of a computer monitor with a plant growing out of it (like what will be in display) and the message, "Discover the hidden garden inside your computer."
  - Back of card mentions show special (when they bring the card to the booth)

- Partner with local greenhouse to promote and provide plants for the display in exchange for signage and mention in promotions
- Place fliers at partner greenhouse and in local libraries

Attractions:
- Software demo (hands-on) as well as virtual-to-real photo transitions on screen

Giveaways:
- Printout of an attendee's basic design (allowing only 2 to 3 minutes each so they can't do a complete design)
- CD jewel case with flower-shaped CD demo (very limited; include virtual-to-real photos), promotional catalog of other software
- A seed packet (provided by the partner greenhouse)

Media Relations:
- Send press releases to local newspapers, garden magazines, and TV stations

Follow-Up:
- For purchasers, send a thank-you e-mail ("48"), followed by a note on a floral card with a gift certificate to use at the partner greenhouse ("10"), and then call in 2 to 3 weeks to answer any technical questions ("30")
- For prospects, send a brochure with a special offer to receive a greenhouse gift certificate with the purchase of software

ROI:
DigiCrayon had an estimated 1,050 visitors to their booth; 425 of whom were qualified leads. Of those, 175 placed orders, totalling $6,125.

Calculations:

Percent of Goal achieved (sales): 175 ÷ 250 = 70%
Percent of Goal achieved (leads): 425 ÷ 500 = 85%
Cost per qualified lead: $4,000 ÷ 425 = $9.41
Cost per sale made: $4,000 ÷ 175 = $22.86
Cost per impression: $4,000 ÷ 1,050 = $3.81
% of leads converted to sales: 175 ÷ 425 = 41%
% of total attendees attracted: 425 ÷ 18,000 = 2.4%
Sales income per dollar spent: $6,125 ÷ $4,000 =$1.53
Media impressions: 15,000 (2 local gardening magazines)
15,000 x 2.5 (pass-alongs) = 37,500 impressions

Lessons Learned:

Although DigiCrayon didn't make either their sales or leads goal, they were pleased with their first experience at the Home & Garden Show. The partnership with the greenhouse was very successful – the green house picked up a number of new customers due to the coupons. Next time, DigiCrayon will consider getting a larger booth and actually displaying with the green house (they feel that if their booth had been larger, more people would have stopped; traffic stayed very heavy throughout the show).

Fictional Case Study: Purple Carrot Press

Scenario:

A children's book publisher wants to showcase their new line of collateral materials (stuffed toys, games, puzzles); two main characters to feature: Sunny the Frog and Alyssa

Show:

Regional book and toy retailers' show with an estimated 7,000 attendees over two days (14 hours); a vertical trade show

Exhibit:

20' x 30' island booth

Goals:

Out of those who stop at the booth:
- Gain 550 leads (stores to possibly carry products)
- Sign up 100 new retailers within 30 days of show
- Gain media coverage (at least one TV and one print)

Breakdown:

40 leads per hour

Budget:

$10,000	Space rental
$ 7,500	Booth design & new graphics
$8,000	Show services
$5,000	Shipping
$6,500	Travel & lodging (10 staffers)
$8,000	Promotions
$2,500	Staffing
$2,500	Misc. expenses
$50,000	

Theme:

"More than Just a Story"

Booth Design:
- Use existing island display frame with new graphics (oversized reproductions of actual storybook pages)
- Four product display stations (with a mix of books and other items; connected to giant book with arches); each has storage underneath
- Incorporate giant puzzles on floor
- Create an experience with sounds of frogs and insects, or books on tape being played over product stations (using plexiglass sound domes)
- Add scents of grass for Sunny the Frog and tea party items (cookies, lemonade) for Alyssa

Staff:
- At least eight staffers in booth at all times, one at each product station and one at each "page" of the giant book

Attire:
- Men wear green shirts and black pants (to blend with Sunny's stories); Women wear rose shirts and black skirts (to blend with Alyssa's stories)

Opening Lines:
- "When was the last time you played a game?"
- "Who's your favorite frog?" (Sunny, of course!)
- "How do you bring a book to life?"

Qualifying:
- Find out the prospect's type and size of store, target demographics, and who is in charge of buying decisions

Pre-Show Promotions:
- Send a series of mailers to clients and prospects
  - Mailer one: Postcard of Sunny the Frog
  - Mailer two: Postcard of Alyssa

- Mailer three: 3-D pop-up "book" with a card invitation inside (with instructions to bring the completed card to the booth; also to save the pop-up for a surprise to come later)

Attractions:
- Costumed characters of Sunny the Frog and Alyssa on hand in the booth (alternating 20 minutes on and off) to pose for photos with attendees in front of the giant book
- One product station demonstrating the new Sunny game, with attendees encouraged to participate
- Special offer: Opportunity to host costume character in the client's store with a $1,000 wholesale order placed within 30 days of the show

Giveaways:
- Photos (fit in pre-show mailer pop-up book as frame)
- Drawing for $500 of bonus merchandise (using pre-show lead cards)

Media Relations:
Send press releases to trade magazines and local TV stations; also take the characters to a local children's hospital the day before the show opens

Follow-Up:
- For all leads, send an e-mail thank-you and announce the winner of the $500 of free products ("48")
- For hot prospects, personally call them within a week to finalize their order; for warm leads, send them a catalog or brochure ("10")
- For new clients, send a welcome letter "signed" by Alyssa and Sunny: "We're looking forward to playing with your young customers!" ("30")
- Send a post-show survey via e-mail or fax to all leads about 4 to 6 weeks after the show

ROI:

- Purple Carrot Press had an estimated 1,800 visitors to their booth, 650 of whom were qualified leads. Of those, 176 placed orders within the first 30 days, totalling $130,000. (46 qualified for the costume visits.)

Calculations:

Percent of Goal achieved (leads): 650 ÷ 550 = 118%
Percent of Goal achieved (sales): 176 ÷ 100 = 176%
Cost per qualified lead: $50,000 ÷ 650 = $76.92
Cost per impression: $50,000 ÷ 1,800 = $27.77
% of leads converted to sales: 176 ÷ 650 = 27%
% of total attendees attracted: 650 ÷ 7,830 = 8.3%
Sales income per dollar spent:
    $130,000 ÷ $50,000 = $2.60
Media impressions:
    150,000 (local paper) + 10,000 (industry magazine) = 160,000 x 2.5 (pass-alongs) = 400,000 impressions

Lessons Learned:

Purple Carrot was thrilled with the response to their booth! However, at times, it was more than they could handle (there were lines of nearly 50 people at times). Next time, more staff will be assigned (10 or 12 instead of 8). The special offer and photo opportunites proved to be a terrific draw.

Purple Carrot Press
Staff Evaluation of Show

Name of Show: Regional Book & Toy   **Date:** July 2001
Location: Chicago's Navy Pier
Registered Att.: 7,830   **Est. Booth Att.:** 1,800

Please rate the following: (5 = excellent, 1 = poor)

Booth Logistics (size, traffic flow)	5 4 3 2 1
Pre-show promotion effectiveness	5 4 3 2 1
Booth attraction effectiveness	5 4 3 2 1
Staffing (number, scheduling)	5 4 3 2 1
Booth staff training/daily team meetings	5 4 3 2 1
Appropriate amount of literature & supplies	5 4 3 2 1
Booth traffic quality	5 4 3 2 1
quantity	5 4 3 2 1
Lead gathering system used	5 4 3 2 1
Overall impressions of show	5 4 3 2 1

Compare our booth to competitors (effectiveness & traffic)
❏ Ours much better   ❏ Ours slightly better   ❏ About the same
❏ Ours slightly worse   ❏ Ours much worse

Follow Up: Have all contacts from this show been followed up?   ❏ Yes   ❏ No

Should we exhibit at this show next year?   ❏ Yes   ❏ No

Comments: _____
_____

Name: _____

"The greatest
thing in this
world is not
so much where
we are, but in
what direction
we are moving."

– Oliver Wendell
Holmes

Adding On

Not every construction project ends once the roof is on and the paint is dry. Sometimes there are special situations which arise that require a different kind of attention.

Perhaps you're in the position of selling real estate (as a show manager) or rewarding the crew (with booth staff incentives). Maybe you want to show off what you've built with a house-warming (special event) or design alternative housing (road shows or private shows). Just as your exhibit should be a cohesive part of your marketing plan, so should these "extra-curricular" activities. Be sure to keep your message in focus when you're considering any of these special situations.

While the first chapter in this section is written for Show Managers, that doesn't mean that exhibitors can't learn some things as well. The most successful trade shows happen when there is a great working relationship between the exhibitors and Show Management, because a Show Manager's job is ...

More than Selling Real Estate

Many of the same techniques covered in earlier chapters also apply to the show itself: branding (defining your image), marketing (promoting to get the word out), creating an experience, and forging media relations.

Branding Your Show

As the coordinator of a trade show, realize that you're competing with dozens of other shows for an exhibitor's time and money. You have to define what makes your show different from the rest; what do you offer that they don't? A highly targeted audience? Special promotional opportunities or prime media exposure? Show exhibitors how you can help them succeed and they will be there.

Create a personality for your show. Is it high-energy and trendy or classic and elegant? Just like the exhibitor must use their corporate personality to create a theme for the booth, you should use it to position your show in the marketplace. Will your exhibitors and attendees be drawn to a hectic and fun environment, or one that's more educational and high-tech? You've got to make them glad that they spent their time at your show and give them positive experiences to remember. Be innovative! Become known for something unique within your industry or community and it will keep your show from simply becoming a commodity.

Build a relationship with your exhibitors, just like they need to with attendees. Remember to make them feel important (MMFI) and show them the benefits that will be gained with active participation (WIFM). Always thank them and make them feel appreciated.

Once you've developed a unique personality for your show, communicate it in all your materials, beginning with the exhibitor prospectus. Set the tone for an upbeat, trendy show with a glossy, colorful brochure. For a more conservative show, choose subdued colors on classic stock. Include information on your unique audience demographics (using audited data, if at all possible), attendee buying plans, what attendees look for at the show, and how long they spend. Ask the exhibitors what they need to know about the attendees. Provide a list of previous exhibitors and a floor plan (with sold-out spaces marked), as well as a show schedule and travel information. Give them a list of deadlines, including

The Elements of a Show's Image

Visual
- Aisle carpet, pipe and drape, signage, props (check with your decorator, or rent from a local theater)

Technology
- Online show service forms, ISDN lines, laptop rentals, Webcasting

Exhibitor Relations
- Exhibitor prospectus, show manual, accessibility to management on show floor

Speakers/Entertainment
- Spouse or guest programs, educational programs, hospitality events

Attendee Quality
- Partner with industry associations or publications, conduct post-show surveys

Strategic Partners
- Media and sponsors (provide not only added publicity, but can also help add unique elements to the show)

those for early-bird discounts. And don't forget to outline your marketing plans and sponsorship opportunities. All of this information can be easily incorporated into your show's web site.

Did you know?

•➤ The industry average for exhibitor retention is 81% for fixed-location shows and 79% for shows that rotate to different cities. The rate for attendee retention is 76% for fixed-location shows and 68% for rotating shows.

•➤ The average annual growth rate for shows: Attendees – 4%, Exhibit space – 3.1%, Exhibitors – 2.6%. (*Source: Tradeshow Week Magazine survey*)

> As your
> exhibitor
> satisfaction
> rate goes,
> so goes
> your show!

Image-Builders that Create an Experience

In order to design an experience that exhibitors and attendees can't bear to miss, you need to think like people in the entertainment business – especially if your show is geared toward consumers. It must be interactive with such features as live entertainment, educational seminars, and attractions around the show floor. Southern Shows, producers of nearly 20 consumer shows a year, promotes all of their events as participatory with something to appeal to all the senses. People will judge your show by how it makes them feel.

Some other Image-Builders:

• Create unusual entrances or settings that attendees walk through or around to enter your show. The International Housewares Show uses giant props, such as frying pans and electrical outlets, to identify the four separate expos that make up the show at McCormick Place.

• Incorporate signs into the decor all around the show. The International Housewares Show also uses "factoid" signs (reminiscent of the old-fashioned Burma-Shave signs) throughout McCormick, according to Debbie Teschke from the National Housewares Manufacturers Association.

• Provide seating areas around the show for attendees to rest. The Home Builders Association of Greater Kansas City partners with the Parks & Recreation Department to create park-like settings throughout Bartle Hall Convention Center. Some of these parks even include gazebos and waterfalls.

• Raise the bar for exhibitors by judging the booths. Criteria could include pre-show promotions, booth design, staff performance, in-booth attractions, and more. Southern Shows actually grades all of their booths (see chart below), with F's losing space at future shows and D's losing priority. The second morning of the show, exhibitors attend a breakfast where awards are

Exhibit Judging/Grading Criteria for Commercial Exhibits at Southern Shows

Design	40 points	90 - 100	A+
Creative use		80 - 90	A
of space	20	70 - 80	B
Appropriate theme	20	60 - 70	C
Appeal (color,		50 - 60	D
texture)	20	Under 50	F

presented to the winning booths, based on exhibit appeal, accessibility, interaction of booth staff, and other criteria. You could also have "Secret Shoppers" who walk the aisles to critique performance.

Building Relationships with Exhibitors

Your relationship with an exhibitor doesn't end once they've signed a contract – that's only the beginning! Coach them through the entire process. Just like you can't expect a teenager to be a good driver without any driving lessons, you can't expect exhibitors to be successful without your help! Work as a team.

Begin by surveying attendees to find out their needs, and then communicate their answers to exhibitors. Next, help them set realistic goals, based on your audience demographic information. Don't just tell them your show attracts 25,000 attendees! Since so many numbers have been overinflated through the years, exhibitors don't trust them anymore. If your show has never been audited, work off your registration information or post-show surveys and create a breakdown of the types of buyers who attend your show.

Provide assistance with lead gathering or lead management, booth staff training, and exhibit design (Southern Shows sends photos of good examples). Partner with experts in each of these areas if you don't have the expertise within your

 Benefits of Show Audits

•◆ Gives you a competitive advantage over other shows that aren't audited

•◆ Verifies the quality of your audience

•◆ Provides a level of confidence in your show and establishes you as an industry leader
— Paula Fauth,
ABC Expomark

(Note: Information from an audit is not publicly disseminated. For more on Show Audits, see Chapter 2.)

management team. Offer pre-show promotional tools, including online promotions (more on this later in the chapter). Streamline paperwork, or offer forms online. Consider assembling an exhibitor advisory council, made up of about a dozen seasoned and new exhibitors, to act as liaisons and answer questions.

The Florida Restaurant Association has a Floor Captain Program, where volunteer members of the Association walk the show floor as the eyes and ears of Show Management. Although a part of their job is to report rule violations, "the Floor Captains' role is more proactive than punitive, acting as an ambassador," according to Ann Eyster of the FRA. The Association also has a Board Visitation Program, where each Board member is assigned a certain number of booths to visit. They interview exhibitors to find out questions and comments about the show. This information is used to improve for future shows.

 Promotions Tool Kit for Exhibitors

•➤ Pre-registered attendee list

•➤ Logo sheets (for inserting into existing materials)

•➤ Order forms for free promotional materials or guest passes

•➤ Promotional pieces, such as brochures, fliers, "Save the Date" postcards, or "See us in booth #___" stickers

•➤ Tips on writing press releases (or provide templates), designing press kits, and creating a media list; also include information about the press room

•➤ Publicity forms (ask exhibitors about new product announcements, special events or other news); also forms to request a press conference (offer on a first-come, first-serve basis)

While having Board liasions is a great strategy, ideally someone from Show Management should also visit with every exhibitor. Ask them for feedback and then act on it as soon as possible. Provide a mentoring program, matching first-time exhibiting companies with long-time, reliable exhibitors. Offer exhibitor "perks," like a classy lounge area, a special exhibitor parking area with a shuttle provided, or members of your team going around on a golf cart during setup and offer free soft drinks. All of these things will be seen as "value-added" and help to improve an exhibitor's experience at your show.

If exhibitors have a bad show, guess who they blame? That's right – Show Management! They don't even stop to consider that they neglected to read the Exhibitor Manual (less than 10% do), do any promotions, or train their booth staff.

The solution? Educate your exhibitors! Help them plan interactive booth activities to draw people in. Offer consultations with first time exhibitors on everything from exhibit design to media relations. Communicate often with all your exhibitors via faxes, phone calls, e-mail or regular mailings. Have a year-round periodic newsletter that comes out about every six weeks to keep them updated on show news, as well as provide tips for improving their exhibit.

Perhaps the most important part of exhibitor education is holding a free exhibitor workshop. Schedule it anywhere from one to four months before the show – you can't expect to hold it two hours before the show opens and see the same results! Invite your GSC, as well as show service providers, exhibit designers and other vendors to participate. Include a member of the host city's CVB to present local entertainment options. Offer special VIP incentives to those

Make your Exhibitor Manual more user-friendly by putting it online or on a CD-ROM. Include printable forms and templates.

who attend, such as special discounts on services. Topics to cover include: logistics, audience demographics (what to expect), pre-show planning and promotions (give them an outline of your promotional and media plans), exhibit design, booth staffing, and lead management. If your exhibitors come from all across the country,

Exhibitor Manual Contents

- Table of contents
- Checklists/Deadline schedule
- Spell out what's included (or not) in a basic booth space
- All service order forms and GSC info
- Move-in and move-out information
- Show hours and complete schedule
- Floor plan and preliminary exhibitor list
- Show rules and regulations
- Housing and registration forms
- Labor information
- Shipping and drayage information
- Tip sheets, including display design and booth staffing
- Lead system information and follow-up tips
- Sponsorship and advertising information
- Promotional plans
- Press information (including how to sign up for a press conference)
- Awards information (such as "Best Booth")
- Resource list

consider holding several regional workshops to make it more convenient for them.

Although many show managers have been afraid of being replaced by <u>virtual shows</u>, that really isn't the case. Actually, a virtual show is a great added promotional tool when used correctly.

Using the Show's Web Site to Inform Year-Round

For Exhibitors:
- Timeline/checklist with links to show service providers
- First-time exhibitors' section with FAQs and Show Rules and Regulations
- Setup information and move-in schedule
- Lead gathering system information/lead management tips
- Easily accessible contact information

For All Attendees:
- Searchable database of exhibitors with a schedule builder (works much like an online "shopping cart" to make a list of exhibitors to visit)
- Capture complete attendee demographic information with online registration (or a printable registration form)
- 360-degree photos of the previous show floor or streaming video clips
- Educational program information with speaker bios
- Hotel and travel info (with links to the local CVB, as well as air and hotel sites)
- Periodic attendee chats; allow questions to be submitted for seminar sessions
- Follow-up with session handouts, media coverage, photos, etc.
- Sell related merchandise (such as audio or video tapes of educational sessions)

The idea is to create a community, both before and after the show, so the actual show experience can be enhanced. A successful web site should be interactive, easily navigated, and constantly updated. This will help to encourage repeat visits, giving both your show and exhibitors more exposure.

Did you know?

➹ 63% of all trade shows have a Web site.
➹ Of those, only about half offer online registration and only 45% offer links to exhibitors. (*Source: CEIR Report #MC40*)

> The more prepared and professional your exhibitors are, the better the image of your show.

Making the Most of Sponsorships

Sponsorships are important because they offer added exposure and get people into the sponsor's booth. Sponsorships can also be used to create unique experiences, such as hospitality events. Structured correctly, sponsorships will benefit everyone – exhibitors, attendees and Show Management. When designing sponsorship packages, be sure to offer different levels to give everyone an equal opportunity. Work with exhibitors to customize sponsorship packages that meet their needs. Outline what costs are covered and what aren't (such as producing signs or tote bags). And spell out the benefits they will receive, such as logo/name recognition, credits in the program or directory, complimentary VIP passes, articles in the attendee newsletter, or web site banners. Take photos of sponsored events, areas or signs and send copies, along with thank-you notes, to sponsors after the show.

Giving Attendees What They Want

When you're planning for your show, keep in mind that the exhibitors aren't your only customers. You've got to make sure your show appeals to attendees too. People are busier today than ever before. You've got to get them excited about spending their time and money to come to your show.

 Sponsorships: Beyond the Basics

Besides the typical banners, product locators, floor decals, hospitality events, and bags, try some of these ideas:

- Awards banquet
- Educational seminars
- Press Room
- Lounge for speakers, exhibitors or VIPs
- Cyber Café
- Shuttle buses or valet parking
- Special area within show (i.e. food court)
- Pocket planners (to schedule appointments with exhibitors)
- Jumbotron or marquee messages
- Postcard racks
- Phone cards
- Espresso cart (moves around show floor to be near sponsors' booths)
- Hotel key cards (specially printed credit card-style keys for official show hotel)
- Tabletop graphics in food court
- Conference CD-ROM with session handouts and exhibitor list
- Room drops (limit number of companies per night)

Cross-promote
your show
with related
associations,
publications,
business-to-
business Web
sites, and
e-zines to
help get the
word out.

One of the biggest complaints from exhibitors is that they don't see enough qualified buyers, regardless of total traffic numbers. In order to combat this problem, ask exhibitors who they would most like to see at the show. Have each exhibitor give you 10 to 20 names, then send those people VIP passes. You could even create a special VIP program, where, in addition to the free passes, those special guests receive bonuses at the show, such as a VIP lounge or special exhibit hall hours just for them.

Shows being held in New York City can take advantage of a special Convention Delegate Pass Program, sponsored by American Express and the NYCVB. Attendees can take advantage of special discounts at area restaurants, theaters and attractions just by presenting their badge. Lists of participating venues can be included in registration packets or on the show's web site.

Attendees also want a strong educational program. Even if your show doesn't have an educational conference *per se*, you can host informational sessions on the show floor, with guest speakers or demonstrations by exhibitors. Understand what types of information the attendees are looking for (educational vs. motivational) and ask those who chose not to attend in the past what they'd most like to see (you should also ask what types of exhibits they are interested in).

Did you know?

•◦ 83% of attendees use pre-show information to plan their visit.
•◦ 75% arrive with a preset agenda. (*Source: CEIR Report #MC12*)

By offering pre-show agenda planning on your web site, you can provide a very important service for time-crunched attendees. The Hospitality Design Expo, a show that attracts over 9,000 designers and decorators of hotels and cruise ships, provides a Personal Itinerary Planner on the Web site. Attendees can create a "shopping list" of exhibitors with products they want to see, and can include notes about what questions they want to ask. Since contact information is included in the planner, an attendee could make arrangements for a private appointment, if they wish.

How NOT to Run a Show

(The following is a true story of one show. However, names have been omitted to protect the guilty.)

As the show opened, some exhibitors were still waiting for tables to be delivered that they had pre-ordered. Then, just before a presentation on the main stage, Show Management called for a cherry picker to hang a banner (this was several hours into the show).

The high-dollar keynote speaker was mysteriously scheduled for the last hour the show was open. If the intent was to get people to stay, it failed miserably. As usual, exhibitors started tearing down nearly two hours before the show closed, so all through the keynote there were clackety carts, beeping forklifts, and squeaking dollies going back and forth around the stage area.

About 15 minutes before close, the house lights started going down. The speaker couldn't bear it any longer. "What's the deal with these people?" he asked with agitation. But being a true professional, he continued his presentation in the dimly-lit show hall.

After the show closed, there was supposedly an after-hours reception, but there was no one left to attend! Can you imagine how upset that sponsor must have been?

Other "Perks" for Attendees:
- Shuttle to all official hotels
- Business center/Cyber Café
- Interactive competition (such as a student design contest or a cook-off)
- "Ugly Bathroom" contest (or other such category) at consumer shows (attendees bring in photos to be judged; winners receive a "makeover")
- Children's activity area at consumer shows

Making Friends with the Media

In order for your exhibitors to have positive media relations, you need to create a positive environment for members of the press. Create a media section on your show's Web site where you can post press releases (and summaries of educational sessions after the show). Let the media e-mail questions about the show, schedule interviews, or fill out a form requesting advance information. Prior to the show, send them a schedule of all press conferences.

At the show, it's important to have a press room that is easily accessible, and not just a lounge! Have members of your staff on hand to answer questions about the show and schedule one-on-one interviews or photo opportunities with exhibitors (furnish a small conference area for these). Provide a Cyber Café with computer workstations or hookups for their laptops. Keep a supply of exhibitors' press kits and show dailies on hand, as well as audio tapes or summaries of educational sessions. Post a master schedule of all press conferences and product announcements. You can even offer to ship items (such as press kits) back to their office for free.

Just like the exhibitors, you need to build relationships with the media. Meet with editors and keep in contact regularly (not just when you're

---

Hire a professional photographer to take photos of the show and educational sessions for use in future promotions. Include it as an added service for your exhibitors so they can have photos taken of their booths.

promoting a show). Invite them to participate in a panel discussion or some other part of your overall event. And don't forget to thank them.

Vocabulary

Virtual show: the online version of a trade show; allows people to "visit" an exhibitor before or after the actual show is held, and can also offer other opportunities for those who are unable to attend, such as live Webcasts from the show floor

Resources

ABC Expomark
847-879-8272
www.abcexpomark.com

NYC & Company (NYCVB)
212-484-1200
www.nycvisit.com

"Originality
is the only
thing that
counts. But the
originator uses
material and
ideas that
occur round
him and pass
through him.
And out of
his experience
comes the
original
creation."

– George Gershwin

Housewarmings

With more and more exhibitors doing special events off the show floor, the challenge is always, "What can we do to really stand out?" Simply booking a hotel hospitality suite just doesn't cut it anymore.

One option is to sponsor an official hospitality event at the show. Often, there are numerous luncheons, receptions and banquets to choose from. While hosting one of these events simplifies your responsibilities, there are some drawbacks (see chart). You might also want to consider creating a special event all your own.

The road to a successful event starts by choosing your date and knowing what (and who) you're competing against, suggests Jani Lauvrak Lee, Director of Operations for Seattle VIP Services, a destination management company. "You have to be realistic in your expectations and head count, then plan accordingly." And keep in mind that most show organizers won't allow exhibitors to host events at the same time as scheduled show activities.

Select your theme, and then set the tone with your invitation so people will know what to expect. Decide on a budget (typically between 5 percent and 10 percent of your overall exhibit budget) and plan the event so that there will be a little something for everybody. "More people want interactive events," says Lee. "That makes it good for both introverts and extroverts, and also promotes networking."

Make sure you have enough staff to work the event.

Be sure they understand that they're not there to party!

The focus of any special event should be net-working. It should not be a three-hour sales pitch. Use the event to build goodwill, and follow up later with your message. If you've done a good job hosting the event, your message will be well received.

Large-Scale Events

Planning a mega-event? While it takes a lot of coordinating, you can host successful events for hundreds of people. Just be sure you don't invite more guests than you can afford to entertain.

Pros & Cons of Sponsoring Official Trade Show Events

	Pros	Cons
Attendance	More people will attend your event because it will be open to all	People will attend who you don't necessarily want there
Value	You get more bang for your buck because the association or other sponsors pay some of the costs	You don't get all the credit
Control	You won't have to handle all the tasks and responsibilities	You cannot have total control over the style and format
Recognition	Your name will be publicized	You'll share recognition with others
Competition	You won't have other events to compete with	Your competition will attend your event

Tips used with permission of Penny Ripple, owner of The Ripple Effect

Bayer Corporation held a Veterans Day event for about 300 people in two hangars at the Pima Air and Space Museum near Tucson. Guests were transported to the museum early to view the outdoor exhibits before the evening's events began. Inside the hangars, the jets were lit with uplights and costumed mannequins sat in the cockpits. The staff dressed in service uniforms of the 1940s and 1950s and there was even a General Patton look-alike to mingle with the crowd as period music played. "It was a very patriotic crowd," says Cathy Ewing, CMP and Corporate Meeting Manager with Bayer.

Bayer has also hosted 1,200 people in Anaheim on board the Queen Mary. Guests arrived by motor coach and were treated to three types of music throughout the ship, as well as multiple food stations. The evening concluded with fireworks off the fantail.

An estimated 1,800 people attended a Gilligan's Island party around the Tropicana Hotel pool in Las Vegas. It was a twist on the traditional scavenger hunt, with guests receiving keys to a treasure chest for each activity they completed, including doing the hula or singing the Gilligan's Island theme song. Even if their key didn't open the treasure chest, they received prizes based on the number of keys collected.

Using Available Facilities

One way to trim costs is to host your event in a popular entertainment venue. You'll save not only time on planning and setup, but also money on decorations and activities. Another benefit of using a location unique to your host city is that it gives people a chance to experience the culture of that city. Since trade show attendees' schedules are often jam-packed, with little time

> Many of the elements of planning you exhibit also apply to special events. For example, send your invitations about one month prior to the event. You might also require that they check in at your booth to pick up an actual event ticket.

for sightseeing, they may be more likely to attend your event if they can see someplace new.

At the 1999 Holiday Showcase in Chicago, the Detroit Convention and Visitors Bureau hosted a special evening that started with each client being picked up (with their chosen guest) in a limousine and transported to the Shedd Aquarium for dinner. Later, the attendees traveled by motor coach to a theater performance, where they were seated in a VIP suite. The evening ended with another limousine ride home.

Detroit's meeting planner Jennifer Neal says that the key in planning such an event is to be

---

Setting Measurable Objectives for Events: Some Examples

•• Each staff member will meet with one new prospect (train your staff how to identify and approach these prospects)
•• Each staff member will spend time with at least three different guests (create interactivity opportunities that politely force guests to meet staff)
•• Attract 10 top prospects (have guests pick up something with their name on it before leaving)
•• Retain guests longer into the event (have them particpate in an activity that will earn them a parting gift and note the pickup time)

These are *not* measurable goals:
•• Mix and mingle
•• Increase name awareness
•• Show appreciation to clients
•• Reward employees

Tips used with permission of Penny Ripple,
owner of The Ripple Effect

organized and to delegate the duties. "We had a form for each of the 19 limo drivers listing pickup and drop off addresses and times," she says. "Then we created a spreadsheet with contact information and details for each one."

Bayer Corporation's Cathy Ewing discovered a unique venue at the Agricultural Hall of Fame Museum in Bonner Springs, Kan. On the museum's grounds is a small old-style town, called Farmtown, USA, that is not open to the public. Guests were greeted by the town sheriff and interacted with character actors at each building. There was even a cowboy poet in the barn, with hay bales for audience seating. "There are lots of quaint little places that you don't normally think of, but with a little creativity, it can be a unique event," Ewing advises.

Las Vegas offers more than its share of unusual venues. One popular choice is Liberace's home, where his original staff members give tours, and of course guests are entertained by a Liberace look-alike. Jaki Baskow, owner of Baskow and Associates, a DMC and talent agency, has also held events at the nearby NASCAR track. Guests can ride along with a driver, or even take a turn behind the wheel. For those who can't decide on just one venue, Baskow can organize a Vegas scavenger hunt, with busses taking guests all over town following clues and snapping photos. Some of the favorite stops include Wayne Newton's ranch and an "Elvis wedding." The

Ideas to Keep Costs Down

- Invite suppliers or non-competing companies to co-host an event with you
- Limit the event to a two-hour time frame and provide only light hors d'oeuvres
- Utilize drink tickets, then provide a cash bar
- Invite only your top prospects and clients
- Host the event some where other than a hotel

hunt ends with a party at the Fremont Street Experience, the computer-generated light and sound show in downtown Vegas.

Some of the most successful events hosted by the Atlanta Convention & Visitors Bureau have been held in exclusive private homes. Not only is the setting more cachet than a hotel ballroom, but "people are basically nosy" and want to get a look inside, according to Rick Myers, Senior Vice President of Trade Shows. The ACVB once held an event at a mansion in Los Angeles, guest hosted by actor Tim Conway. Other events have been held at John Wayne's home and at a private ranch near Houston. Myers suggests contacting destination management companies in your show city to find private homes that are available to rent. Keep the guest list very small and elite (stay under capacity to keep it comfortable) and make sure you have the necessary insurance coverage. One way to avoid trouble is to have the homeowners there for the party, Myers advises.

> If you must have music at your event, keep the volume low enough so people can still talk to each other. The main purpose is networking, remember?

 ## Using Music at Your Events

In order to perform any published music at a public event, you must obtain a performance license from either ASCAP (American Society of Composers, Authors & Publishers) or BMI (Broadcast Music Inc.). Each of these two organizations act as a one-stop clearinghouse for obtaining performance rights and paying royalties. They represent thousands of music creators. Fees are based on the type of use and size of the audience. Another option is to obtain a "blanket license" that entitles you to use all of the songs in that organization's repertoire for one annual fee.

Upscale department stores (such as Neiman Marcus or Nordstrom), can be used for after-hours receptions with different food stations and entertainment on each floor. Arrangements are made for the store to keep one or two departments open for shopping during the reception (guests are informed ahead of time what areas will be open).

Many groups have taken advantage of a location's movie or celebrity history with theme tours. For example, in Chicago, there's the "Untouchables" gangster tour; in Memphis, an Elvis or blues tour.

Non-profit facilities are often inexpensive to rent. Always be sure to ask about what services are included in the rental fee, as well as any restrictions (i.e. alcohol, smoking, exclusive caterers, etc.). If guests will be driving themselves to the location, make sure there is adequate parking. Better yet, why not use a special method of transportation that will help set the theme?

 **Ideas for Unique Venues**

- Riverboat or yacht (think sunset cruise)
- Country estate or mansion
- Park, garden or botanical center
- Beach or marina
- Private suite at football or baseball stadium (even if there's no game!)
- Zoo, aquarium or planetarium
- Art gallery or museum
- Concert hall or theatre
- Landmark buildings or historic sites
- Airport VIP lounge or cruise ship lounge (while docked)
- Air Force Base (think "Top Gun")
- Navy aircraft carrier

For example, for a Wild West barbecue, use a hay wagon or stagecoach. For a military-themed gathering, pick up the guests in a Humvee or helicopter. If your event is in New Orleans, or another Southern plantation area, use a horse and carriage.

Tips for Choosing a Theme

- Use current hot topics (but avoid overused themes)
- Adapt to the situation
- Keep it simple (and easily understood)
- Make it consistent with your company culture (Is it elegant, high-tech or sporty?)
- Coordinate with both budget and location
- Carry it out through the invitations, menu, decor, giveaways, etc.

Consider hiring a photographer or videographer to record your event. Have a location set up to take portraits of guests, incorporating the event theme or the celebrity host or look-alike. Include your company name on the finished photos and *voila!* – Instant memorabilia!

Themed Events

Being in an entertainment smorgasbord like Las Vegas, Jaki Baskow never has a shortage of ideas for theme events. Her basic principle of event planning? "Every party should be an experience. The key is to have a good time and make it memorable. But remember ... it's all about your product!"

Be specific in telling guests what to wear. If costumes or formal wear are expected, be sure to let them know in the invitation. Consider giving guests something to wear that reinforces the theme (and bears your logo). You could hand out straw hats with bands bearing your company name at a western barbecue, or windbreakers at a ball game or other outdoor event.

A sporting goods company exhibiting at the Crown Center Exhibit Hall in Kansas City held a Sports Night with virtual reality golf, tricycle races, and a mini race car track. The atmosphere was similar to a carnival, according to Tyler Adkins, Sales Manager at the Hyatt Regency Crown Center. They brightened the space with balloons and different colors of carpet and served ballpark-style foods.

One exhibitor in Las Vegas held a Winter Wonderland party in a hotel ballroom when it was 120 degrees outside! There were Canadian Mounties mingling with the crowd and even an indoor ice rink. Attendees nearly forgot they were in the middle of the desert!

Exhibitors have taken advantage of the closing night of a show by having a slumber party. Held either in a ballroom or an entire floor of the hotel, the event featured massages, manicures, and of course food. Guests received nightshirts with the sponsor's logo on them and even took a turn at karaoke.

The Dallas CVB transformed a warehouse into a 1960s biker haven with Harley-Davidson parts (collected from two local Harley clubs) as decorations and centerpieces. Guests were surprised by riding to the event in a procession of Harleys, led by four police officers. The hosts, as well as the drivers, dressed in traditional Harley gear, and guests were given temporary tattoos bearing the official Dallas logo. When using speciality transportation, Dallas CVB Event Planner Colleen Rickenbacher, CMP, cautions to always have guests sign a waiver before the event, as well as having backup transportation for those who choose not to participate. But she quickly adds that no one refused to ride on a Harley!

Whether you're planning an exclusive gathering for ten VIPs or a huge event for a thousand, don't lose sight of your message. Special events provide the opportunity to meet with clients and prospects in a more relaxed environment than on the show floor. There is more opportunity for in-depth conversation and rapport-building.

> **Have guests include their hotel name in their RSVP. Then you can create a small room drop gift with a reminder the night before the event to generate anticipation.**
>
> - Penny Ripple,
> The Ripple Effect

Plan a truly special event, and people will be talking about both it and your company for weeks afterwards.

Resources

Atlanta CVB
404-577-3293
www.atlanta.com

ASCAP
www.ascap.com

Baskow & Associates
702-733-7818
www.baskow.com

BMI
www.bmi.com

Crown Center Exhibit Hall
800-215-8222
www.crowncenter.com/
exhibit_hall.html

Dallas CVB
214-746-6688
www.dallascvb.com

Detroit CVB
800-225-5389
www.visitdetroit.com

Seattle VIP Services
206-623-2090
www.seavip.com

The Ripple Effect
904-454-3491
www.therippleffect.com

Alternative Housing   15

Although the number of trade shows held each year continues to increase, there has been an interesting trend developing over the past few years. Many exhibitors are now choosing to "take the show on the road."

This trend has developed partly because of rising costs to exhibit, as well as the high level of competition on the show floor, according to Allen Reichard of The Freeman Companies. With a private event, you have a more controlled environment – you can focus on a very select audience and deliver a more targeted message with much bigger "bang," he says.

It's important to keep your name in front of customers and prospects between shows. It's also important that you maintain high visibility, even in slow economic times, when many of your clients will be trimming the number of shows that they attend. Private shows or road shows can be effective when used in addition to, or in place of, a traditional exhibit.

These private events take many forms. Wholesalers invite their retail clients to visit exhibits of their partner suppliers and manufacturers. Franchisers sponsor an event for all their franchisees or dealers. Many companies host clients in their own facility, providing manufacturing plant tours and educational opportunities. (Some even charge people to attend training sessions!) Other companies host in-house trade shows, showcasing various product lines. This can be even more effective when other companies are invited to exhibit, especially ven-

> **Private shows are the ultimate example of a vertical show.**

dors or business partners with complementary products.

Lawson Software, a provider of e-business solutions, has been holding a Conference & User Exchange (CUE) for more than 15 years, with approximately 5,000 attendees now paying up to

Private Events vs. Traditional Trade Shows

	Pros	Cons
Traditional Shows	Provides high visibility in industry; builds brand awareness in the market	Just one of many exhibits; not in control of who sees exhibit
Private Shows	Builds on previous relationship; can be a follow-up to a traditional show for groups of highly qualified prospects; can control timing of message	High risk; very expensive and labor-intensive; not always an immediate return on investment
Road Shows	Goes to them instead of waiting for them to come to you; allows more control over environment; provides one-on-one time with prospects and clients with no competition	Responsible for all planning and expenses (can cost $500,000 or more, depending on length of tour)

$1,400 each to attend the four-day event. Lawson provides educational sessions presented by their employees, customers and business partners. In addition to their own exhibits, Lawson includes about 80 suppliers and strategic partners who share an interest in the same client base. Each of these partners sets up exhibits that are basically case studies in the use of Lawson Software, showing practical applications for each type of solution.

One of the benefits of hosting your own private show is that it builds confidence by providing a personal touch, according to Josi Fredstrup of Conference Coordinators. A client can meet face-to-face with staff members that they deal with on a regular basis via phone and e-mail. Relationships are built and customer loyalty increases. Another benefit is that you can more easily measure your ROI with a direct correlation of sales resulting from the event over a period of time.

Planning a private show or road show is much like putting on a special event. It takes a huge amount of planning and coordination. Fredstrup advises companies not to try and do everything themselves. Catering, audio/visual, security and logistics can all be outsourced to event management professionals and exhibit industry suppliers. And private shows are not cheap to do. As your own show manager, you'll be responsible for all of the costs (unless you charge others to participate, like Lawson Software does). So before you forge ahead, ask if there's any other way you can accomplish your goals.

Why Road Shows?

For companies whose focus is on business-to-business sales, small regional private expos may offer the best solution. Road shows, on the other

> "If your reason is not to show product but presence, you may be a candidate for a private event."
>
> - Allen Reichard, The Freeman Companies

hand, are more suited for consumer-focused companies that need to get their message out to the masses. Perhaps the most recognized (and longest-running) road show is the Oscar Mayer Weinermobile, which was first launched in 1936. Now, thousands of people pose for photos beside the 27-foot rolling hot dog each year.

Designing a road show, or mobile exhibit, can take on many forms. While these events typically center around some kind of vehicle with dynamic graphics on it (usually a 48-foot to 53-foot climate-controlled trailer), what is included varies widely. Some companies choose to create

Checklist for Deciding to Go on the Road

Why do you want to do it?

❏ Your product is too large or too complex to demonstrate in field sales or at a show

❏ You want control over the environment and attendee list

❏ You need to meet with prospects who won't or can't attend a trade show

❏ You don't want to compete with all the other exhibits, especially your competitors

Who will attend?
❏ Clients
❏ Prospects
❏ Distributors
❏ End users

What is your goal?
❏ Generate media exposure
❏ Build relationships with clients/prospects
❏ Educate users

a mobile classroom, complete with a conference table, acoustic ceiling, and a retractable video screen. This "mini-auditorium" can be used for training, campus recruiting, stockholder meetings, or educational presentations, according to Harry Kurtz of Mobility Resource Associates Inc., a company that builds customized mobile display trailers. By using trailers with expandable sides, MRA can turn a basic design into a 1,000-square-foot space, he says.

Some companies are focused on creating an immersive environment, where prospects and customers can get involved in hands-on demonstrations. Others want a rolling museum filled with various learning stations. Still others want a high-tech virtual reality center to draw huge crowds at festivals and sporting events. The bottom line for every mobile exhibit is that it must draw people in, grab their attention, and get them interacting with the host company.

Road shows work best when end users need to "see it to believe it," because thousands can be exposed to the product by touching, tasting or testing it. Users also have the opportunity to ask questions one-on-one in a more relaxed environment.

Lands' End used a 14-city road show to bring body scanning technology to the masses. Consumers entered a dark room wearing a special bodysuit and 360-degree measurements were taken. Less than a minute after the scan was completed, their "virtual model" was downloaded into the Lands' End web site for future shopping "try-ons." A partnership with the My Virtual Model software company and the makers of the body scanning machine, the goal of the tour was to "help people create the most accurate measurements for their virtual model," according to Beverly Holmes, Director of

If you can't get your customers to the show, take the show to them!

Road shows really aren't new – they're just a new spin on the old idea of a peddler and his wagon.

Communications for Lands' End. She estimates that 3,000 people were scanned during the tour (about 100 per day).

Dockers decided to use a road show as a "way to express that we're more than just pants," says Kelly Moore. So, they created the Style@Work tour, featuring wardrobe stylists from Vogue and InStyle magazines offering business casual advice and wardrobe makeovers for busy professionals. Visitors have the opportunity to ask a professional stylist what is right for them. The truck, which includes dressing rooms, mirrors and a runway, creates an interactive experience, as well as reinforcing the Dockers advertising.

When Ericsson wanted to demonstrate the array of products they offer regarding Mobile Internet

 **Thinking Outside the Box ... Way Outside!**

A road show doesn't have to take place in a 50-foot trailer. Companies have commissioned everything from Humvees to VW Beetles as mobile exhibits. One unique tour consists of two Kisses and a Hug!

Hershey's designed the Kissmobile for the 90th birthday of their famous Kisses in 1997. One of the three giant fiberglass candies serves as the cab, while the other two store equipment and a supply of thousands of Hershey's Kisses. Each of the three Kissmobiles travels approximately 50,000 miles per year, going to over 170 children's hospitals. One of the two drivers dresses up in the Hershey's Kiss costume to entertain the kids.

It's not difficult for the Kissmobile to attract attention. Drivers have a hard time even stopping for gas without being mobbed!

and Next Generation Networks, they decided to take it to their customers' backyards. Working from requests by telecommunications clients, the double-wide expandable trailer pulled into more than 30 cities its first year. The biggest advantage of this road show, according to Jennifer Ziegler, Ericsson's Manager of Event Marketing, is that most of the people who attend don't go to any industry trade shows. This way, more of their clients can see the technology in action. Typically, the first day of the tour starts with an executive meeting for VIPs, followed by open tours for all of the client's employees. Lunch is served and sometimes, at the close of the final day, a hospitality event is held with live entertainment (the unique trailer has a hospitality area on the roof). Inside the trailer, five different "solutions" areas are showcased, featuring Mobile Internet and Next Generation Networks technology such as video conferencing, mobile gaming, and "road warrior" Internet access.

Because your trailer is a rolling billboard, it must be kept spotless at all times!

Not only does a mobile exhibit become a giant rolling billboard (with a potential of 10 million impressions a year), but it is also a great public relations tool. Successful road show coordinators make publicity a big part of the tour, incorporating a "media blitz" the first day in each new city. The tour's traveling experts can be interviewed on morning radio and TV shows. Many companies incorporate a local cause, such as collecting for the Second Harvest National Food Bank Network (Oscar Mayer's "Share the Smiles" program provided more than 18 million meals to Americans in need) or raising money for the Children's Miracle Network (Hershey's Kissmobile), giving another reason for media coverage.

One element of the Dockers tour is a clothing drive. As visitors come to get educated in the art

Try Out a Trailer

One great way to test a road show's potential is to lease a vehicle. For example, if a company wanted to do a product launch, the leased trailer could still be customized both inside and out, then taken to a few cities to judge audience response. The cost would be less than one large exhibit at a major trade show.

of business casual wear, they bring their used clothing to donate to local charities. The bins fill up every day, according to Moore.

The key to a successful road show is to go where your target audience is. For consumer products, that often means public venues in a central or downtown location. Lands' End took their trailer to Wall Street and Times Square. On Fridays, Dockers sets up their show in a city's business district (on Saturdays, they set up where their local retail partner is located). The challenge? Because of the size of the vehicle, those ideal venues may sometimes be difficult to access.

Effective road shows also develop partnerships in each local area. The Buick "Drive with Confidence" and "Golf Experience" tours cross the country, cooperating with local Buick dealers in each city. The tours typically tie in with PGA tournaments, charity events and festivals, according to Bill Bissmeyer of Performance Marketing Group, the tour coordinator. PGA pros are often on hand to help give pointers for a visitor's golf swing (which can be computer-analyzed in the "Golf Experience" tour). In the "Drive with Confidence" tour, visitors experience a unique, 360° virtual-reality coast-to-coast test drive narrated by Ben Crenshaw. Along the way, the visual experience is enhanced with realistic sounds and smells, including lilacs, evergreen trees and fresh-cut grass. Each person in the simulator can enjoy their own unique and memorable experience.

Tracking Results on the Road

Just like stationary trade show exhibits, road shows need to have some method of measuring results. If your goal is to build a client database, you must have a system for gathering leads.

Buick dealers report a phenomenal response to the "Drive with Confidence" tour, which runs five trucks for 48 weeks a year. Even dealers in

 Road Show Logistics

Always wanted to be a Show Manager? If you decide to do a road show, you will be. All of the following tasks will now be on your shoulders. If it seems overwhelming, just remember, there are a wealth of people out there who can help you. (See some suggestions in the Resource Guide.)

●◆ Arrange for venues in high-traffic areas (for consumer products) and obtain necessary permits with local authorities

●◆ Plan most efficient routes from city to city, creating a daily itinerary

●◆ Keep costs within budget (in addition to the trailer itself, there are expenses for gas, salaries, hotel and food, promotions, site fees and more)

●◆ Generate publicity in each city

●◆ Hire talent to staff the exhibit (or send existing staff) as well as a driver, who must be able to answer basic ques tions about the company and capture lead information when needed

●◆ Design the exhibit, inside and out

small towns can have 300 to 600 people on their lots while the tour is on site. Tying in with the golf theme, visitors are invited to participate in a "Scorecard Challenge," where they answer questions about the cars. The answers are easily discovered as the visitor interacts with the car, opening the trunk, glove box, and so on, Bissmeyer says. By turning in their scorecards, participants may receive prizes like a phone card, disposable camera, or sleeve of golf balls. The leads are then compiled for the dealer and can be easily tracked to determine ROI, based on future sales.

Although they haven't tracked use of the online model by individual participants, Holmes says they do know that those who utilize the Lands' End My Virtual Model are more frequent (and higher volume) purchasers. The tour served its purpose by generating lots of interest in the new technology (whether or not the visitors ever intend to use their model) and by gaining valuable feedback from a variety of people. The company also received attention in both consumer and apparel industry media.

Ericsson contracted with a third party company to measure the initial results of their "Drive to 3G" (Third Generation Wireless) tour. Visitors were asked to participate in an exit survey, which was done using specially-equipped PDAs. An overwhelming majority of guests rated the overall experience as "Excellent," and indicated they had increased understanding of Ericsson's mobile Internet solutions "a lot."

But along with positive feedback comes room for improvement. Ericsson discovered that there is such a thing as being too popular, with most of the negative comments stemming from over-crowding. Because they offered a free box lunch, the trailer was jam-packed over the lunch hour,

---

Be sure you check out any regulations that might affect your road show. For example, since Lands' End is a catalog company, they aren't able to do a road show in a state where they don't have an existing store or charge sales tax.

yet nearly empty at other times. One possible solution? Offer incentives to people who come at non-peak times or provide a sign-up sheet. Another idea is to have a staffer positioned at the entrance to function as "crowd control," allowing only a certain number of people into the trailer at one time. One revision Ericsson has made using the attendees' feedback is to create short (15-minute) small-group presentations on 3-G technology, followed by a tour.

When considering whether to do a private show or road show, remember that you are crossing the line from being strictly an exhibitor to being your own show manager. With that role comes an entirely new set of details and responsibilities. But if you plan an integrated campaign and aren't afraid to ask for help, you can find yourself generating a huge amount of buzz ... coast to coast!

Resources

Conference Coordinators
877-346-9074
www.ccievents.com

The Freeman Companies
214-670-9000
www.freemanco.com

Mobility Resource Associates
800-676-3520
www.goMRA.com

"Appreciation
is the oil
that makes the
wheels of
progress turn."

– Anonymous

Rewarding the Crew

It's a basic tenet of human nature: People love to be winners!

A good staff incentive program can help to create that sense of winning. It can also more than double staff performance. Incentives provide a sense of achievement and a desire to exceed expectations. Since many people are not self-motivated, an incentive program can give them that extra bit of encouragement needed.

You can choose to reward positive behavior (actions; can be based on customer feedback surveys) or results (such as number of sales or leads). Either way, it's important to reward both the team and the individuals. Remember it must be fair to all the staffers. If you reward only individuals, someone will certainly feel left out and unappreciated. By rewarding only the team, those who work the hardest may resent the "loafers" who still are rewarded when the team achieves the goal. By rewarding both, you allow everyone to celebrate the victory, and still give extra incentive to achieve individually. Yet another idea is to make it a competition between shifts.

The most successful way to reward is with an open-ended program (everyone who meet goals wins). Achievers at each level are rewarded accordingly, with the biggest prizes reserved for those at the top level. This creates a greater sense of equality than close-ended programs where only a few people receive awards.

How do you create a successful booth staff

> "You'll never get the best from employees by trying to build a fire under them – you've got to build a fire within them."
>
> – Bob Nelson, owner of Nelson Motivation and author of 1001 Ways to Reward Employees

incentive program? You have to have a game plan. Planning a program doesn't happen overnight. Spend some time designing creative rewards that are fair, and you will see a significant increase in trade show results.

Rate your staff! Hire "mystery shoppers" to visit your booth and evaluate the staff's performance.

Setting Up Your Incentive Program

1. Establish Your Objectives

Before you can design an incentive program, you must first determine what your company's objectives are for the show. Is it to distribute samples? Generate leads? Make sales? Each of these objectives requires a different type of reward program. You should focus on the one objective that is your main target and then develop realistic and measurable goals for the team. (But then you did that back in Chapter 1, right?)

For example, if your company objective is to generate 300 leads, then use that as your ultimate target. (Just a word of caution: count only qualified leads, so staffers aren't signing up everyone who wanders by your booth!) Once you have your team goal, break it down for individuals. If you have six staffers, each would have a goal of 50 leads. Make each staff member accountable.

Now that you have defined your goals, you must communicate them, along with how results will be measured. Decide on the method you will use for both the team and individuals.

2. Determine Budget

How much is it worth to meet your objectives? What will you be missing if they're not met?

Consider your budget limitations, but be realistic. If you think a budget of $100 will be enough to reward a staff of six, you're in for an unfortunate surprise. On the other hand, you don't need to set aside $10,000 either! Look at your total number of staffers involved, as well as your expected results. Determine how much you will earn by meeting your objectives and use that as a guideline to create a "bonus" for the entire staff.

A general rule suggested by the Promotional Products Association International is to spend 75 to 80 percent of your incentive program budget on the actual awards, and the remainder on

> "Many know how to flatter; few understand how to give praise."
>
> - Greek Proverb

 Creative Booth Staff Rewards

- ◗◗ Arrange for VIP treatment while at the show (like a special dinner with industry leaders)
- ◗◗ Photo recognition (in company newsletter or intranet)
- ◗◗ Lunch back at the office (or hold a party for the team)
- ◗◗ Day off/half day off
- ◗◗ Massage (to recover from all that time in the booth!)
- ◗◗ Night on the town with spouse/guest
- ◗◗ Items for their family, like home electronics or toys for the kids
- ◗◗ Gift certificate for shopping
- ◗◗ Corporate logo items
- ◗◗ Point system, redeemable for various prizes
- ◗◗ Merchandise (electronics, unique gift items, luggage, etc.)
- ◗◗ Services (maid service, personal chef, etc.)
- ◗◗ Travel

(For even more ideas on staff incentives, check out *1001 Ways to Reward Employees*, by Bob Nelson)

administration and promotion of the program.

3. Select the Awards

Your awards must be something that will motivate your staffers, so why not get their input in the planning stages? They may point you to rewards that management would never have thought of. The awards should be in line with your company image (for example, a fun-loving company might want to reward with a paintball adventure). Also, choose incentives appropriate to the performance expected.

> "All behavior is a function of its consequences – you get what you reward."
>
> - Bob Nelson

Be creative! Build your incentive program around a central theme. Choose an idea that is easily recognizable and lends itself to graphics and metaphors. Sports is often easy to incorporate as a theme. (See the examples at the end of this chapter.)

Remember WIFM – "What's in it for me?" While cash is an easy answer, it's not the most effective motivator. Instead consider merchandise, entertainment or services. The more unique and exciting the reward, the longer it will be remembered.

Consider including the family in the reward, especially if your staff spends a lot time on the road. Then it becomes a thank you for not only your staff member's hard work, but also his or her family's sacrifice.

4. Communicate and Administer Program

Companies often do some kind of kickoff for their staff, as a morale booster. Get the team motivated to perform. This can be held several days prior to the show in the home office. Then, just before the show opens, hold another meeting on the show floor. At the end of each day, hold briefings to track progress.

Send "teasers" to staff before the official announcement of the program to build excitement (much like pre-show promotions!). Communications can be via newsletters, fliers, or e-mail. You could also include some kind of gift relating to the contest.

The key is to communicate clearly and often. Make sure everyone understands the company goals, as well as rules for the incentive program. The more frequent the communication, the more excitement you generate.

 Don't Lose Focus!

Never use a contest as a sympathy tool with attendees! They don't care whether you're winning a steak dinner or not. They only want to know what's in it for them. Besides, what good does it do to win if you don't have any qualified leads to follow up on later?

One good idea is to use a point system. The PPAI suggests using 200 points per dollar of prize value. For example, for a $25 prize, a staffer must accumulate 5,000 points. Then set point values for each achievement. For instance: qualified leads, 200 points each; on-site sales, 1,000 points each (or it can be based on the size of the sale). If your goal is to increase the sales of a specific product line, consider giving bonus points for leads or sales of those items. (Be sure to award points to all team member working together to qualify a lead.)

Anticipate what might go wrong. Cover thoroughly how points are accumulated and how prizes will be awarded. Be specific about what counts as a qualified lead. Give each staffer a printed list of prizes with points needed, as well as how many points they will earn for each action.

Other Ways to Motivate Staff

- Have staffers vote for the "Staffer of the Day
- Do nightly hotel room drops with notes of encouragement for staff
- Reward them for the number of appointments they set up from pre-show promotions

---

5. Celebrate Success

Be sure to recognize both the team and the individuals with timely rewards. Announce team and individual results daily at the show. Post results back at the office after the show so staffers can get extra recognition from peers. Always award prizes promptly, either at the close of the show or at a ceremony back at the office.

6. Analyze Results

How do you know if your incentive program was successful? First of all, were your company's objectives achieved? Determine how much your sales increased. If no sales were made at the show, then track sales resulting from the show within the first six months. Look at results compared to last year's show or another comparable show.

Were your rewards appropriate motivators for the staff? Ask for feedback. If the results were motivating to some staffers, but not others, find out why. Is there something else that would be more universal? Or should you consider having multiple rewards?

Job satisfaction in the new century is as much about recognition as it is salary. When you design an incentive program for your staff, it's a win-win for everyone. The staff is more productive at the show, and they are well rewarded for their actions. Encourage them to all become MVPs.

Go team!

Example Program: XYZ Manufacturing

Goal: To sell 75 of new $395 machine

Budget: Sales when goal is reached = $29,625
Budget for program = $1,500 ($1200 for prizes, $300 for
promotion/admin.)

Theme: Football Playoffs

Prizes: Tickets for two to local NFL team home game (20,000 points)
NFL team stadium blanket (10,000 points)
NFL team apparel (5,000 points)
Tailgate party for entire team if sales goal is reached

Point System: Sales of any product = 600 points ("Touchdown")
Sales of featured product = 200 bonus points ("Two-point
conversion")
Qualified leads = 300 points ("Field Goal")

Communications: Kick off with "Pep Rally" and give each participant
mini-footballs with company logo on them. Have daily
"Huddles" at the show to track progress on a "scoreboard."

Resources

Nelson Motivation
619-673-0690
www.nelson-motivation.com

**Promotional Products
Association International (PPAI)**
972-252-0404
www.ppa.org

"Three things
are to be
looked to
in a building:
that it stand on
the right spot;
that it be
securely
founded;
that it be
successfully
executed."

- Goethe

Remodels, Renovations and Repairs

Now that you've read this book cover to cover, you think you're done, right?

Wrong! Your exhibit image is progressive: it's never done. This book is just a starting point to get you moving in the right direction. You must constantly evaluate whether your exhibit was successful at a show, and decide what needs to be done to make it better. Just like a house will occasionally need basic repairs, you must be willing to make adjustments in your exhibiting plan.

Sometimes, it's more than a simple repair. Maybe you realize that your exhibit (or your methods) have become stale, and are in need of some remodeling. You don't need to start all over. Just tweak the elements that are no longer presenting the image you want.

If, after finishing this book, you come to the conclusion that your exhibiting plan needs to be taken back to square one, you now have the tools to do a complete renovation. Begin at the beginning with your goals and budget and rebuild your exhibit plan piece by piece. And keep in mind, there's no one set blueprint to follow because each company is unique.

In this book, you've seen numerous examples of how to get creative with every element of your exhibit. Pick your favorite ideas and determine how to put them to work to make your company stand out from the crowd.

> "Even if you're on the right track, you'll get run over if you just sit there."
>
> - Will Rogers

As Allen Reichard of The Freeman Companies says, today's trade shows are not about showing wares. "It's now about reinforcing brand by creating an environment. You've got to create the image of a leader."

> **"Nothing is so contagious as enthusiasm."**
>
> – Samuel Taylor Coleridge

Back in the "Dark Ages" (the early 1990s), when a product development cycle was between 12 and 36 months, companies could schedule their product launches to coincide with major trade shows. Now, with a high-tech, high-speed global economy, that's just not realistic anymore. Coordinating an exhibit now involves much more than basic logistics. It has to be a complete marketing package. Focus on marketing your brand, and then delegate much of the logistics to exhibit industry suppliers.

Reichard notes that a new relationship is developing between exhibitors and suppliers. "There's a higher level of trust and confidence because [the supplier] has become a part of the [exhibitor's] company and the overall process," he says. Ultimately, exhibiting success is the product of a three-way relationship between the exhibitors, suppliers and show management. With all three working toward the same goal, it's awesome to see the results!

The "Secret" Ingredient

Whoever said that success is just showing up never worked a trade show. You've got to design a blueprint to follow, assemble the right tools, and build on a solid foundation. But no matter how thoroughly you've planned, there is still one more key to success: attitude. It has been said that with the right attitude you can do everything wrong and still succeed, but with the wrong attitude, you can do everything right and fail. When hard work meets a positive attitude, anything is possible.

TradeShowTips Online, Issue #17: "Lessons Learned from the 2000 U.S. Presidential Election"

I know what you're thinking ... "How can this wacky election possibly have anything to do with trade show exhibiting?" But please bear with me – there are several lessons to be learned!

Lesson 1: If you don't build a strong image for yourself, don't expect to emerge a clear winner above your competition.
Perhaps the whole election snafu might never have happened if the two candidates had been able to build better images for themselves. If you don't establish a reason for prospects and customers (or voters) to choose you, you might as well not show up.

Lesson 2: Don't run down the competition.
Building a strong image doesn't mean doing so at someone else's expense. How often have you gone into the voting booth without a clear-cut picture of any of the candidates? Sure, you know a lot about them, but it's all negative things that came from their opponents. While the 2000 campaign may not have been incredibly vicious, the weeks of bitter fighting after election night made some people say they no longer wanted either candidate. Remember: If you have to resort to tearing someone else down to build yourself up, you're creating a very shaky foundation and it can come back to haunt you.

Lesson 3: Have a contingency plan for what might go wrong.
Don't get caught with equipment that doesn't work, or people who don't know what they're doing. When you're preparing for a show, run some "what if" scenarios. Be prepared to handle more visitors to your booth than you really expect. Do a "dress rehearsal": assemble your booth ahead of time to make sure you know what you're doing, role-play with your staff to handle objections, and know how to run any equipment you may be using.

If you fail to learn these lessons, you may find yourself in a "living nightmare," just like the Presidential candidates!

Call on a Professional

Associations

Association of Female Exhibit Managers & Convention Organizers (AFEMCO)
1595 Spring Hill Rd., Suite 330
Vienna, VA 22182
703-506-3280
703-506-3266 fax

Center for Exhibition Industry Research (CEIR)
2301 South Lake Shore Drive, Suite E1002
Chicago, IL 60616
312-808-CEIR
312-949-3472 fax
www.ceir.org
Membership-based organization that provides research reports to help exhibitors be more effective; can call to order reports mentioned throughout this book

Computer Event Marketing Association (CEMA)
490 Boston Post Rd.
Sudbury, MA 01776
978-443-3330
978-443-4715 fax

Convention Industry Council (CIC)
10200 West 44th Ave., Suite 310
Wheat Ridge, CO 80033-2840
303-422-8522
303-422-8894 fax

Exhibit Designers & Producers Association (EDPA)
5775-G Peachtree-Dunwoody Rd., Suite 500
Atlanta, GA 30342
404-303-7310
404-252-0774 fax
www.edpa.com

Exhibitor Appointed Contractors Association (EACA)
2214 NW 5th St.
Bend, OR 97701-1211
541-317-8768
541-317-8749 fax
www.eaca.com

Exposition Service Contractors Association (ESCA)
2920 N. Green Valley Pkwy., Suite 414
Henderson, NV 89014-0413
702-319-9561
702-450-7732 fax
www.esca.org

Healthcare Convention & Exhibitors Association (HCEA)
5775-G Peachtree-Dunwoody Rd., Suite 500
Atlanta, GA 30342
404-252-3663
404-252-0774 fax
www.hcea.org

International Association for Exhibition Management (IAEM)
5001 LBJ Freeway, Suite 350
Dallas, TX 75244
972-458-8002
792-458-8119 fax
www.iaem.org

International Association of Assembly Managers (IAAM)
635 Fritz
Coppell, TX 75019-4442
972-255-8020
972-255-9582 fax
www.iaam.org

International Association of Convention & Visitors Bureaus (IACVB)
2025 M Street, NW, Suite 500
Washington, DC 20036
202-296-7888
202-296-7889 fax
www.iacvb.org

Meeting Professionals International (MPI)
4455 LBJ Freeway, Suite 1200
Dallas, TX 75244-5903
972-702-3000
972-702-3070 fax
www.mpiweb.org

National Association of Consumer Shows (NACS)
147 SE 102nd Ave.
Portland, OR 97216
503-253-0832
503-253-9172 fax
www.publicshows.com

Professional Convention Management Association (PCMA)
2301 South Lake Shore Drive, Suite 1001
Chicago, IL 60616-1419
312-423-7262
312-423-7222 fax

Society of Independent Show Organizers (SISO)
7000 W. Southwest Hwy.
Chicago, IL 60645
877-YES-SISO
www.siso.org

Trade Show Exhibitor's Association
2301 South Lake Shore Dr.,
    Suite 1005
Chicago, IL 60616
312-842-8732
312-842-8744 fax
www.tsea.org

Publications

Convene
PO Box 663
Ardsley, NY 10502
914-693-6246
914-693-7005 fax
www.pcma.org

Event Solutions
3300 N. Central Ave., Suite
    2500
Phoenix, AZ 85012
480-990-1101
480-990-0819 fax
www.event-solutions.com

Exhibit City News
1675 E. Desert Inn Road
Las Vegas, NV 89109
702-309-8023
702-309-8027 fax
www.exhibitcitynews.com

Exhibit Marketing (Eaton Hall Publishing)
256 Columbia Turnpike
Florham Park, NJ 07932
973-514-5900
973-514-5977 fax

EXHIBITOR Magazine
206 S. Broadway, Suite 745
Rochester, MN 55904
507-289-6556
507-289-5253 fax
www.exhibitornet.com

EXPO Magazine
11600 College Blvd.
Overland Park, KS 66210
913-469-1185
913-469-0806 fax
www.expoweb.com

Expotential
PO Box 899
Hermosa Beach, CA 90254-
    0899
310-798-1268
310-406-8628 fax
www.expotentialmag.com

Meeting News
1 Penn Plaza, 10th Floor
New York, NY 10119
212-714-1300
212-279-3949 fax

Meetings & Conventions
500 Plaza Dr.
Secaucus, NJ 09094
201-902-1700
201-319-1796 fax
www.meetings-
    conventions.com

Potentials
50 S. Ninth St.
Minneapolis, MN 55402
612-333-0471
612-333-6526 fax
www.potentialsmag.com

Sales & Marketing Management
770 Broadway
New York, NY 10003
www.salesandmarketing.com

Sales & Marketing Strategies & News
211 W. State St., PO Box 197
Rockford, IL 61105
800-435-2937
815-963-7773 fax
www.salesandmarketingmag
.com

SAM Magazine
117 W. Micheltorena St.,
Suite C
Santa Barbara, CA 93101
805-965-5858
805-963-1143 fax
www.sammag.com

Successful Meetings
355 Park Ave. S.
New York, NY 10010-1789
800-898-3874
www.successmtgs.com

Trade Show Ideas
2301 South Lake Shore Dr.,
Suite 1005
Chicago, IL 60616
312-842-8732
312-842-8744 fax
www.tsea.org

Tradeshow & Exhibit Manager
1150 Yale St., Suite 12
Santa Monica, CA 90403
310-828-1309
310-829-1169 fax

Tradeshow Week
5700 Wilshire Blvd., #120
Los Angeles, CA 90036-5804
323-965-5300
323-965-5304 fax
www.TradeshowWeek.com

Audio/Visual

AVW Audio Visual (The Freeman Companies)
1421 W. Mockingbird
Dallas, TX 75247
214-670-9000
214-670-9101 fax
www.freemanco.com
Services include equipment rental as well as special effects and logistical support

BigEdison.com
3805 N Oak Trafficway
Kansas City, MO 64116
816-455-2933
www.bigedison.com
Produces live Web cam broadcasts, 360-degree virtual tours, and CD-ROMs

Flying Beyond
1604 Blossom Hill Road
San Jose, CA 95124
408-266-3220
408-266-3262 fax
www.fbeyond.com
Trade show theater, interactive

CD-ROMs, booth promotions and other marketing communications

MC²
3 Alpine Ct.
Chestnut Ridge, NY 10977
800-537-8073
845-578-1625 fax
www.mc-2online.com
Multimedia products, kiosks

Skytron
16 Technology Dr., Suite 169
Irvine, CA 92618
949-753-8500
949-753-8504 fax
www.skytron.com
360-degree video display with speaker system on a tower or suspended from ceiling

V-Lite
209 E Alameda Ave., Suite 203
Burbank, CA 91502
800-937-6268
www.v-lite.com
Lightweight video tapes that are easily mailed (1/3 of the weight of a standard video cassette)

Video Post
2029 Wyandotte
Kansas City, MO 64108
800-804-5434
816-531-1957 fax
www.videopostkc.com
Full-service digital production company; HDTV, audio, video, graphics and animation

Apparel

Bankers Advertising Company
PO Box 2060
Iowa City, IA 52240
319-354-1020
319-338-0943 fax
www.bankersadvertising.com
Logo apparel

Lands' End
6 Lands' End Lane
Dodgeville, WI 53595
800-338-2000
800-965-3329 fax
www.landsend.com
Logo apparel

MTI Marketing
6190 Yarrow Dr.
Carlsbad, CA 92009
760-603-9600
760-603-1640 fax
www.MTImarketing.com
Logo apparel

Ralph Marlin
PO Box 999
Hartland, WI 53029-0999
800-922-8437
414-369-8810 fax
www.ralphmarlin.com
Creative ties and scarves, including popular cartoon characters; also offers custom designs

Wood Associates
2360 Bering Dr.
San Jose, CA 95131
408-965-4996
408-965-4999 fax

www.woodteam.com
Logo apparel

Computer Rental

National Micro Rentals
28 Abeel Rd.
Monroe Township, NJ 08831
800-637-2496
609-395-7142 fax
www.nmrrents.com

PCR (Personal Computer Rentals)
211 College Rd. East
Princeton, NJ 08540
800-473-6872
609-720-0814 fax
www.pcrrent.com

Exhibit Design

Abex Display Systems
7101 Fair Ave
North Hollywood, CA 91605
818-764-5126
818-503-9955 fax
www.abex.com
*Manufactures custom modular
and portable exhibits*

Chicago Exhibit Productions
755 Remington Blvd.
Bolingbrook, IL 60440
800-626-0579
630-378-0214 fax
www.cepinc.com
Custom and portable exhibits

Dersé Exhibits
1234 N. 62nd St.
Milwaukee, WI 53213
800-562-2300

414-257-3798 fax
www.derseexhibits.com
*Full service exhibit manufacturer
from design and construction to
installation*

Display Designs
55 Progress Way, Unit #4
Jackson, NJ 09527
800-220-3882
732-928-3141 fax
www.displaydesigns1.com
Custom exhibits that are interactive environments

DrapeLine
1196 32nd Street
Oakland, CA 94608
888-942-7177
www.johnmurray.com/6.htm
Custom painted backdrops

George P. Johnson Co.
50 Oliver St.
North Boston, MA 02356
310-965-4300
310-965-4660 fax
www.gpjco.com
Integrated event marketing

Jackson Shrub Supply Inc.
11505 Vanowen St.
North Hollywood, CA 91605
818-982-0100
818-982-1310 fax
Hollywood prop designer

K&S International Inc.
600 Wheeling Rd.
Wheeling, IL 60090
847-229-0202
847-229-1001 fax

www.tradeshowflooring.com
Soft exhibit flooring

MC²
3 Alpine Ct.
Chestnut Ridge, NY 10977
800-537-8073
845-578-1625 fax
www.mc-2online.com
Custom exhibits

Nimlok Co.
7420 NW Lehigh Ave.
Niles, IL 60714
800-233-8870
847-647-2044 fax
www.nimlok.com
Compact pop-up designs, custom modular and tabletops

Nomadic Display
7400 Fullerton Rd., Suite 134
Springfield, VA 22153
800-732-9395
703-866-1869 fax
www.nomadicdisplay.com
Compact pop-up designs, custom modular

StagePlan Design & Display
1101 Battersby Ave.
Enumclaw, WA 98022
888-249-9553
360-825-5435 fax
www.stageplan.com
Metal and wood fabrication for displays, furnishings, and mobile exhibits

The Freeman Companies
1421 W. Mockingbird
Dallas, TX 75247

214-670-9000
214-670-9101 fax
www.freemanco.com
Designs ranging from portable displays to custom exhibits

Transformit
33 Sanford Dr.
Gorham, ME 04038
207-856-9911
207-856-2353 fax
www.transformitdesign.com
Unique, freestanding or hanging fabric structures

WinnTech Digital Systems
7023 E 12th Terrace
Kansas City, MO 64126
800-WINNTECH
816-333-6545 fax
www.winntech.com
Custom exhibits combining creative materials with innovative technology; also makers of the "Scorpion," a mobile multi-media merchandising unit

Exhibit Design: Lighting

Display Supply & Lighting Inc.
1247 Norwood Ave.
Itasca, IL 60143
800-468-1488
630-285-9670 fax
www.dslgroup.com
Source for display lighting and supply products

Upstaging Inc.
909 Tower Rd.
Mundelein, IL 60060
847-949-4900

847-949-4909 fax
www.upstaging.com
*Full-service source for theatrical
lighting and custom logo and
image projection*

Exhibit Rental

Catalyst Exhibits
675 Industrial Dr.
Cary, IL 60013
877-397-3682
847-462-1589 fax
www.catalystexhibit.com
Exhibit display rentals

Chicago Exhibit Productions
755 Remington Blvd.
Bolingbrook, IL 60440
800-626-0579
630-378-0214 fax
www.cepinc.com
Custom & portable exhibit rentals

Cort Trade Show Furnishings
811 S. Acacia, Suite B
Fullerton, CA 92831
888-576-2967
714-992-2814 fax
www.corttradeshow.com
Furniture rental for any event

MC²
3 Alpine Ct.
Chestnut Ridge, NY 10977
800-537-8073
845-578-1625 fax
www.mc-2online.com
Custom exhibit & A/V rentals

Nimlok Co.
7420 NW Lehigh Ave.

Niles, IL 60714
800-233-8870
847-647-2044 fax
www.nimlok.com
*Compact pop-up designs, custom
modular and tabletops*

The Freeman Companies
1421 W. Mockingbird
Dallas, TX 75247
214-670-9000
214-670-9101 fax
www.freemanco.com
*Rent exhibit displays, carpet and
furniture*

Exhibit Transportation & Shipping

Allied Van Lines
215 W. Diehl Rd
Naperville, IL 60563
630-717-3687
330-717-3900 fax
www.alliedvan.com
*Special Products Showcase fleet
for trade show shipping*

ELITeXPO
610 Supreme Dr.
Bensenville, IL 60106
800-543-5484
630-616-2019 fax
www.elitexpo.com
*Freight transportation in the U.S.
and around the world, specializing
in trade show shipping*

FedEx Custom Critical
2088 S. Arlington Rd.
Akron, OH 44306
800-255-2421

330-724-2007 fax
www.fedexcustomcritical.com
Pick-up and delivery 24/7/365;
same day or next day

Roadway Express Inc.
1077 Gorge Blvd.
Akron, OH 44310
800-257-2837
330-643-6631 fax
www.roadway.com
Shipping provider with exhibit ser-
vice managers onsite (most shows)

The Freeman Companies
1421 W. Mockingbird
Dallas, TX 75247
214-670-9000
214-670-9101 fax
www.freemanco.com
Shipping from small packages to
the entire exhibit

Yellow Freight System
10990 Roe Ave.
Overland Park, KS 66211
913-344-3000
www.yellowfreight.com
Shipping provider with exhibit ser-
vice managers onsite (most shows)

Graphics

Big3D.com
1419 M Street
Fresno, CA 93721
559-233-3380
559-233-3699 fax
www.big3d.com
Lenticular graphics, large color
printing, displays and lightboxes

Custom Color Corporation
300 W. 19th Terr.
Kansas City, MO 64108
800-821-5623
816-842-1498 fax
www.customcolor.com
Photographic and digital services
including graphics, banners, signs,
transparencies and mounting

Great Big Pictures Inc.
1444 E. Washington Ave.
Madison, WI 53703
800-236-8925
608-257-1067 fax
www.gbpinc.com
Large format graphics

UV/FX
171 Pier Ave.
Santa Monica, CA 90405
310-821-2657
310-392-6817 fax
www.uvfx.com
UV-based scenic backdrops that
appear to change from day to
night or between dual images

Lead Management

bCard.net
7962-C Old Georgetown Rd.
Bethesda, MD 20814
800-215-2266
301-654-3760 fax
www.bcard.net
E-marketing technology including:
lead management, incentive pro-
grams, and registration

Clozer
215 Edgehill Rd.

York, PA 17403
877-843-4790
717-843-4790 fax
www.SalesClozer.com
*Custom database that allows
leads to be imported from multiple
sources, then organized, qualified
and managed*

ExpoExchange
1888 N. Market St.
Frederick, MD 21701
800-448-1883
301-662-9411 fax
www.expoexchange.com
*Full service lead management
products*

Innovative Fulfillment Solutions
210 NW Plaza Drive
Kansas City, MO 64150
888-275-3000
816-587-5881 fax
www.ifssolutions.com
*Provides fulfillment services for lit-
erature, samples or products; also
provides tele-center services*

NewLeads
927 E Main Street – Suite 400
Santa Paula, CA 93060
805-933-1922
805-933-1923 fax
www.newleads.com
*Electronic lead gathering with
computer or Palm compatibility*

RippleWare
PO Box 460
High Springs, FL 32643
386-454-3140
386-454-3501 fax

www.rippleware.com
*Windows-based lead management
software; from badge scans to
extensive analysis reports*

Live Presentations
& Demonstrations

Flying Beyond
1604 Blossom Hill Road
San Jose, CA 95124
408-266-3220
408-266-3262 fax
www.fbeyond.com
*Trade show theater, interactive
CD-ROMs, booth promotions and
other marketing communications*

Ham on Rye Technologies
2612 East Ave.
Wildwood, MO 63040
636-458-3232
636-273-5979 fax
www.hamonrye.com/
   tradeshows
*Virtual reality theater – a combi-
nation of live marketing presentation and virtual reality technology
with real-time lead data*

Jack Rouse Associates
1014 Vine St., Suite 1300
Cincinnati, OH 45202
800-733-2025
513-381-2691 fax
www.jackrouse.com
*Full-time staff of writers, design-
ers, musicians and producers to
create memorable presentations*

Promotions & Giveaways

American Slide Chart
PO Box 111
Wheaton, IL 60189
800-323-4433
630-665-3491 fax
www.americanslidechart.com
Produces dimensional mailers, including pop-ups, slide charts and wheel charts

Bagmasters
1160 California Ave.
Corona, CA 92881
800-843-2247
909-280-2410 fax
www.bagmasters.com
Custom logo totes, briefcases, portfolios and other kinds of bags

Bankers Advertising Company
PO Box 2060
Iowa City, IA 52240
319-354-1020
319-338-0943 fax
www.bankersadvertising.com
Provides an array of promotional products for all kinds of budgets

Branders.com
355 Lakeside Dr., Suite 150
Foster City, CA 94404
650-372-5330
650-372-5331 fax
www.branders.com
Provides an array of promotional products for all kinds of budgets

CCL Promotion Group
6133 N. River Rd., Suite 800
Rosemont, IL 60018
800-225-4332
847-384-0336 fax
www.ccllabel.com
Designers of creative promotions, including "ScreenPlay" (interactive game pieces utilizing the Web) and scratch-and-win tickets

Communipak
11160 Olive Blvd.
Creve Coeur, MO 63141
800-844-4180
www.communipak.com
Custom presentation folders; audio, video & software packaging; 3-D direct mailers and more

DeLano Service Inc.
1300 Lincoln Road
Allegan, MI 49010
800-748-0318
616-673-3749 fax
www.delanoservice.com
Makers of "Lunchnotes" notepads in the shape of sandwiches, burgers, pancakes and more

Idea Art
PO Box 291505
Nashville, TN 37229-1505
800-433-2278
800-435-2278 fax
www.ideaart.com
Specialty papers for brochures, cards, invites and more in dozens of themes

InstaFotos
2250 Palm Avenue
San Mateo, CA 94403
800-483-8687

650-571-9319 fax
www.instafotos.com
Instant special event photography

Lands' End
6 Lands' End Lane
Dodgeville, WI 53595
800-338-2000
800-965-3329 fax
www.landsend.com
Custom logo apparel & accessories

Modern Postcard
1675 Faraday Ave.
Carlsbad, CA 92008
800-959-8365
760-431-1939 fax
www.modernpostcard.com
*Full service provider of full-color
cards & in-house mailing services*

MTI Marketing
6190 Yarrow Dr.
Carlsbad, CA 92009
760-603-9600
760-603-1640 fax
www.MTImarketing.com
*Offers a variety of promotional
items for all kinds of budgets,
including the patented Ad-Case (a
cardboard briefcase for attendees)*

Network Music
15150 Avenue of Science
San Diego, CA 92128
800-854-2075
858-485-7598 fax
www.privatelabelcd.com
*Custom-labeled CDs in an assort-
ment of music types*

Paper Direct
PO Box 2970
Colorado Springs, CO
80901-2970
800-272-7377
800-443-2973 fax
www.paperdirect.com
*Specialty papers for brochures,
cards, invites and more in dozens
of themes*

PreciseMedia Services Inc.
909-481-3305
909-481-3405 fax
www.precisemedia.com
*Creative multimedia solutions,
including business-card sized CD-
ROMs*

**Promotional Products
Association International (PPAI)**
3125 Skyway Circle North
Irving, TX 75038-3526
972-252-0404
972-258-3092 fax
www.ppai.org

Ralph Marlin
PO Box 999
Hartland, WI 53029-0999
800-922-8437
414-369-8810 fax
www.ralphmarlin.com
*Creative ties and scarves with pop
culture icons & cartoon characters*

RewardMinutes Phone Cards
Suite 210 – PO Box 611
  Shawnee Sq.
Shawnee-on-Delaware, PA
  18356
800-260-8825

570-420-4578 fax
www.rewardminutes.com
*Pre-paid phone cards that require
recipients to log on to your Web
site to activate the card*

Trip Builder Inc.
1449 Lexington Ave.
New York, NY 10128
800-525-9745
212-410-5639 fax
www.tripbuilder.com
*Supplier of travel guides and fold-
out maps*

Wood Associates
2360 Bering Dr.
San Jose, CA 95131
408-965-4996
408-965-4999 fax
www.woodteam.com
*Variety of promotional products
for all kinds of budgets*

Services for Show Managers

AhhHah!
7138 Little River Turnpike,
    Suite 1210
Annandale, VA 22003
703-573-1314
www.AhhHah.com
*Retrieve, manage and analyze his-
torical data for meeting executives*

Atwood Convention Publishing
11600 College Blvd.
Overland Park, KS 66210
913-469-1100
913-469-0806 fax
www.atwood.com

*Produces show directories, conven-
tion dailies, manuals and handouts on CD-ROMs, and online
show guides; also provides hotel
room drops and sponsorship sales*

b-there.com
11106 Landing Lane
Moon Township, PA 15108
877-828-4373
www.b-there.com
*Attendee relationship manage-
ment system, including housing
and event registration*

Big Badge
1180 Broadway, 5th Floor
New York, NY 10001
212-614-8888
212-614-8884 fax
www.biggroup.com
*Badges ranging from reusable
styles to engraved laminates*

cvent.com
600 New Hampshire Ave., NW
Washington, DC 20037
303-672-5766
202-672-5768 fax
www.cvent.com
*Create event web pages and online
invitations; guests, RSVP 24/7
with secure transactions; track
responses and attendee lists*

EventSource
480 Gate Five Road,
    Studio 115
Sausalito, CA 94965
877-492-9100
415-331-0835 fax
www.eventsource.com

Online RFPs for special events; also handles road show arrangements

Feedback Systems
5826 Naples Plaza
Long Beach, CA 90803
888-463-6494
562-987-3487 fax
www.FeedbackSystems.com
Audience survey kiosks

iConvention.com
5510 Birdcage Street, Suite 200
Citrus Heights, CA 95610
800-382-0682
800-382-0683 fax
www.iConvention.com
Online software for floor plans, registration, scheduling, exhibitor kits, and more

NYC & Company (NYCVB)
810 Seventh Ave.
New York, NY 10019
212-484-1200
www.nycvisit.com
Providers of the Convention Delegate Pass Program

TimeSaver Software
17731 Irvine Blvd., Suite 201A
Tustin, CA 92780
888-877-1100
714-731-2423 fax
www.timesaversoftware.com
RoomViewer program generates event and trade show floor diagrams, as well as calculating needed furniture and equipment

TSOne
PO Box 12221
Overland Park, KS
  66282-2221
888-869-4677
913-498-1195 fax
www.tsone.com
Online exhibitor service manuals

Special Events & Road Shows

Association of Destination Management Executives
3401 Quebec St., Suite 4050
Denver, CO 80207
303-394-3905
www.adme.org
Look up Destination Management Companies by location online

Baskow & Associates
2948 E Russell Road
Las Vegas, NV 89120-2453
702-733-7818
www.baskow.com
Full-service Destination Management Company and talent agency

Conference Coordinators Inc.
1660 S. Alma School Road,
  Suite 203
Mesa, AZ 85202
877-346-9074
480-505-5001 fax
www.ccievents.com
Organizes and implements exhibits, road show, or hospitality events

EventSource
480 Gate Five Road,

Studio 115
Sausalito, CA 94965
877-492-9100
415-331-0835 fax
www.eventsource.com
*Online RFPs for special events;
can also handle road show
arrangements*

**International Special Events
Society**
401 N Michigan Ave.
Chicago, IL 60611-4267
800-688-4737
www.ises.com

MC²
3 Alpine Ct.
Chestnut Ridge, NY 10977
800-537-8073
845-578-1625 fax
www.mc-2online.com
*Marketing and coordination of
road shows and customer events;
also designs interactive E-vites*

Mobility Resource Associates
PO Box 144
St. Clair Shores, MI 48080
800-431-1400
810-445-1516 fax
www.goMRA.com
*Marketing services company spe-
cializing in road show logistics
management and also manufacturers expandable trailers with climate-controlled environments*

The Freeman Companies
1421 W. Mockingbird
Dallas, TX 75247
214-670-9000

214-670-9101 fax
www.freemanco.com
*Coordinate customer events and
road shows*

The Ripple Effect
215 NE 4th St.
High Springs, FL 32643
386-454-3491
386-454-3501 fax
www.therippleffect.com
*Online registration, pre-show pro-
motions, ROI measurement and
themed customer events*

Temporary Booth Staffers

Affinity Models & Talent
873 B Sutter Street
San Francisco, CA 94109
323-525-0577
415-449-3638 fax
www.affinitytalent.com
*Models and talent to serve as
greeters or to host demonstrations*

Baskow & Associates
2948 E Russell Road
Las Vegas, NV 89120-2453
702-733-7818
www.baskow.com
*Models and talent to serve as
greeters or to host demonstrations;
also celebrity look-alikes*

Trade Show Temps
560 S. Main Street, #10W
Los Angeles, CA 90013
213-438-0411
213-438-0410 fax
www.TradeShowTemps.net

Temporary staffers that are experienced in the trade show industry

Trade Show Research

ABC Expomark
900 N. Meacham Rd.
Schaumburg, IL 60173
847-879-8272
847-605-0483 fax
www.abcexpomark.com
Independent, third-party verification of trade show attendance and demographic data

Center for Exhibition Industry Research (CEIR)
2301 S. Lake Shore Dr.,
   Suite E1002
Chicago, IL 60616
312-808-2347
312-949-3472 fax
www.ceir.org
Membership-based organization that provides research reports to help exhibitors be more effective; can call to order reports mentioned throughout this book

Exhibit Surveys Inc.
7 Hendrickson Ave.
Red Bank, NJ 07701
800-224-3170
732-741-5704 fax
www.exhibitsurveys.com
Conducts custom research for trade and consumer expositions, as well as seminars and events

Trade Show & Exhibits Schedule
Bill Communications –
   PO Box 1387

Bellmawr, NJ 08099-1387
856-933-0111
856-931-4115 fax
Directory of trade shows

Tradeshow Week Data Book
5700 Wilshire Blvd., Suite 120
Los Angeles, CA 90036
323-965-2437
323-965-2407 fax
www.tradeshowweek.com
Directory of trade shows

Traffic Builders/ Booth Attractions

20-Minute Vacation
1354 DeHars St.
San Francisco, CA 94107
877-353-9114
415-647-4666 fax
www.20-minutevacation.com
Seated massage stations that attract a crowd and allows marketing message to be delivered during massage

Affinity Models & Talent
873 B Sutter Street
San Francisco, CA 94109
323-525-0577
415-449-3638 fax
www.affinitytalent.com
Models and talent to serve as greeters or to host demonstrations

Baskow & Associates
2948 E Russell Road
Las Vegas, NV 89120-2453
702-733-7818
www.baskow.com
Models and talent to serve as

*greeters or to host demonstrations;
also celebrity look-alikes*

Costume Specialists
211 N Fifth St.
Columbus, OH 43215
614-464-2115
614-464-2114 fax
Costume characters and mascots

Dorfman Museum Figures Inc.
800-634-4873
www.museumfigures.com
*Lifelike figures with microchip
message repeaters; can be customized to look like anyone*

Facemakers Inc.
140 Fifth Street
Savannah, IL 61074
815-273-3944
815-273-3966 fax
www.facemakers
   incorporated.com
Costume characters and mascots

**Funny Faces/Tracy Evans
Productions**
13004 Murphy Rd., Suite 222
Stafford, TX 77477
888-223-8669
281-240-2216 fax
www.tracyevansproductions
   .com
*Video-morphing caricatures; also
provides interactive kiosks and
CD-ROMs*

Ham on Rye Technologies
2612 East Ave.
Wildwood, MO 63040
636-458-3232

636-273-5979 fax
www.hamonrye.com/
   tradeshows
*Virtual reality theater – a combi-
nation of live marketing presentation and virtual reality technology
with real-time lead data*

InstaFotos
2250 Palm Avenue
San Mateo, CA 94403
800-483-8687
650-571-9319 fax
www.instafotos.com
Instant special event photography

Jack Rouse Associates
1014 Vine St., Suite 1300
Cincinnati, OH 45202
800-733-2025
513-381-2691 fax
www.jackrouse.com
*Specializes in creative presentation
of corporate messages*

Ken Courtney
816-228-5531
www.marketing-magic.com
*Corporate magician who includes
company messages in his presentation*

MC²
3 Alpine Ct.
Chestnut Ridge, NY 10977
800-537-8073
845-578-1625 fax
www.mc-2online.com

Pasternak & Associates
13351-D Riverside Drive,
   Suite 381

Sherman Oaks, CA 91423
818-716-5977
818-789-4888 fax
Lt. Columbo look-alike

Sponsorship Services Group
102 Carolina Ct.
Archdale, NC 27263
800-299-6176
336-431-5601 fax
www.ssgmkg.com
Rents racing simulators to use as booth attractions

Tricks of the Trade (Chef Anton)
6213 Sacramento Ave.
Alta Loma, CA 91701
800-679-3859
909-466-4550 fax
www.chefanton.com
Two-time U.S. trick shot champion of pool; provides customized product-focused programs

Miscellaneous Resources

ASCAP
www.ascap.com
Music licensing source

BMI
www.bmi.com
Music licensing source

Gale Group
27500 Drake Road
Farmington Hills, MI 48331
800-877-4253
www.galegroup.com
Produces media directories

Nelson Motivation
11848 Bernardo Plaza Ct.
#210 B
San Diego,CA 92128
619-673-0690
619-673-9031 fax
www.nelson-motivation.com
Management training and consulting company; monthly newsletter "Rewarding Employees"

Network for the Needy (PCMA)
2301 South Lake Shore Dr.,
   Suite 1001
Chicago, IL 60616-1419
312-423-7262
312-423-7222 fax
www.pcma.org
Program that works with exhibitors and show managers to donate leftover food and supplies

TRAQ-IT
PO Box 12221
Overland Park, KS
   66282-2221
888-869-4677
913-498-1195 fax
www.traqit.com
Windows only; tracks budgets, deadlines and payment due dates; generates reports and itineraries

Underwriters Laboratories (UL)
333 Phingsten Rd.
Northbrook, IL 60062
847-272-8800
847-509-6321 fax
www.ul.com
Working with EDPA to develop a standard for displays

Want to Know More?

Blum, Sandra J.: **Designing Direct Mail that Sells**, North Light Books, 1999

Eiseman, Leatrice: **Pantone Guide to Communicating with Color**, Grafix Press, 2000

Falk, Edgar A.: **1001 Ideas to Create Retail Excitement**, Prentice Hall, 1994

Fisher, Donna: **Power Networking**, Mountain Harbour, 1991

Hall, Doug: **Jump Start Your Brain**, Warner Books, 1995

McGinnis, Christopher J.: **The Unofficial Business Traveler's Pocket Guide: 165 Tips Even the Best Business Travelers May Not Know**, McGraw-Hill, 1998

Nelson, Bob: **1001 Ways to Reward Employees**, Workman, 1994

Pine, Joseph and Gilmore, James: **The Experience Economy: Work is Theatre & Every Business a Stage**, Harvard Business School Press, 1999

Pinskey, Raleigh: **101 Ways to Promote Yourself,** Avon Books, 1997

Wolverton, B.C.: **How to Grow Fresh Air: 50 Houseplants that Purify Your Home or Office,** Penguin Books, 1996

Where Can I Find ...

Marlys K. Arnold

About the
Author

With a degree in English and journalism, Marlys Arnold worked for three and a half years as a reporter for the Kansas City Star before launching out with her own business.

Combining her image expertise with real-world marketing experience, Marlys teaches how to "Maximize Your Trade Show Results." She has not only been a trade show exhibitor, but has also organized several expos and events, including a self-improvement weekend for women. Her unique perspective of the trade show industry from many angles allows her to share new insights with both beginning and experienced exhibitors.

A member of TSEA and MPI, Marlys has presented seminars for a number of groups including IAEM, Sprint, and the Home Builders Association of Greater Kansas City. She has been featured in both radio and television interviews, as well as being included in publications from Kansas City to Australia.

She writes two online columns, *TradeShowTips Online* and *The Busy Person's Guide to Trade Show Exhibiting*, and is available for trade show training or consulting. For information, contact:

Marlys K. Arnold, ImageSpecialist
7885 NW Roanridge Road, Suite A
Kansas City, MO 64151
816-746-7888
www.imagespecialist.com
marnold@imagespecialist.com

Notes

Notes

Notes

Notes

Notes

Order Form

Telephone orders: Call 312-777-4002 ext. 7371

Fax orders: Dial 312-777-4002, followed by the Pause key twice, enter 7371, then press Send.

Mail orders: Build a Better Trade Show Image, Tiffany Harbor Productions, PO Box 901808, Kansas City, MO 64190–1808

Quantity Discounts:

1 - 24 books	No discount ($2495)
25 - 99 books	25% ($18.75)
100 - 199 books	30% ($17.50)
200 - 299 books	40% ($15.00)

(Please call for pricing on quantities over 300, or books for resale.)

❑ Please send _____ copies of the book (ISBN #0-9712905-1-2). I understand that I may return any books for a full refund, no questions asked.

Subtotal $_____

Name: _____

Company Name: _____

Address: _____

City, State, Zip: _____

Phone: (____) _____

❑ Please subscribe me to the TradeShowTips Online newsletter, free of charge, at this address: _____@_____

Sales tax: For Missouri addresses, please include 7.1% tax + $ _____

Shipping: $4.50 for the first book and $1.50 for each additional book. + $ _____

Payment: Please enclose payment with order. Payment will be processed at time of shipment.

❑ Check ❑ Money Order ❑ MasterCard ❑ VISA

Order Total $ _____

Card Number _____ Exp. Date ___/___

Name on card: _____ Signature _____

Please make checks payable to Tiffany Harbor Productions.

Order Form

Telephone orders: Call 312-777-4002 ext. 7371

Fax orders: Dial 312-777-4002, followed by the Pause key twice, enter 7371, then press Send.

Mail orders: Build a Better Trade Show Image, Tiffany Harbor Productions, PO Box 901808, Kansas City, MO 64190–1808

Quantity Discounts:

1 - 24 books	No discount ($24.95)
25 - 99 books	25% ($18.75)
100 - 199 books	30% ($17.50)
200 - 299 books	40% ($15.00)

(Please call for pricing on quantities over 300, or books for resale.)

❑ Please send _____ copies of the book (ISBN #0-9712905-1-2). I understand that I may return any books for a full refund, no questions asked.

Subtotal $_____

Name: _____

Company Name: _____

Address: _____

City, State, Zip: _____

Phone: (____) _____

❑ Please subscribe me to the TradeShowTips Online newsletter, free of charge, at this address: _____@_____

Sales tax: For Missouri addresses, please include 7.1% tax + $ _____

Shipping: $4.50 for the first book and $1.50 for each additional book. + $ _____

Payment: Please enclose payment with order. Payment will be processed at time of shipment. _____

❑ Check   ❑ Money Order   ❑ MasterCard   ❑ VISA

Order Total $ _____

Card Number _____ Exp. Date ___/___

Name on card: _____ Signature _____

Please make checks payable to Tiffany Harbor Productions.

Order Form

Telephone orders: Call 312-777-4002 ext. 7371

Fax orders: Dial 312-777-4002, followed by the Pause key twice, enter 7371, then press Send.

Mail orders: Build a Better Trade Show Image, Tiffany Harbor Productions, PO Box 901808, Kansas City, MO 64190–1808

Quantity Discounts:

1 - 24 books	No discount ($24.95)
25 - 99 books	25% ($18.75)
100 - 199 books	30% ($17.50)
200 - 299 books	40% ($15.00)

(Please call for pricing on quantities over 300, or books for resale.)

❏ Please send _____ copies of the book (ISBN #0-9712905-1-2). I understand that I may return any books for a full refund, no questions asked.

Subtotal $_____

Name: _____

Company Name: _____

Address: _____

City, State, Zip: _____

Phone: (____) _____

❏ Please subscribe me to the TradeShowTips Online newsletter, free of charge, at this address: _____@_____

Sales tax: For Missouri addresses, please include 7.1% tax + $ _____

Shipping: $4.50 for the first book and $1.50 for each additional book. + $ _____

Payment: Please enclose payment with order. Payment will be processed at time of shipment.

❏ Check   ❏ Money Order   ❏ MasterCard   ❏ VISA

Order Total $ _____

Card Number _____ Exp. Date ___/___

Name on card: _____ Signature _____

Please make checks payable to Tiffany Harbor Productions.

Order Form

Telephone orders: Call 312-777-4002 ext. 7371

Fax orders: Dial 312-777-4002, followed by the Pause key twice, enter 7371, then press Send.

Mail orders: Build a Better Trade Show Image, Tiffany Harbor Productions, PO Box 901808, Kansas City, MO 64190–1808

Quantity Discounts: 1 - 24 books   No discount ($2495)
25 - 99 books   25% ($1875)
100 - 199 books   30% ($17.50)
200 - 299 books   40% ($15.00)
(Please call for pricing on quantities over 300, or books for resale.)

❑ Please send _____ copies of the book (ISBN #0-9712905-1-2).
I understand that I may return any books for a full refund, no questions asked.

Subtotal $_____

Name: _____

Company Name: _____

Address: _____

City, State, Zip: _____

Phone: (___) _____

❑ Please subscribe me to the TradeShowTips Online newsletter,
free of charge, at this address: _____@_____

Sales tax: For Missouri addresses, please include 7.1% tax + $ _____

Shipping: $4.50 for the first book and
$1.50 for each additional book.   + $ _____

Payment: Please enclose payment with order.
Payment will be processed at time of shipment.   —————
❑ Check   ❑ Money Order   ❑ MasterCard   ❑ VISA
Order Total $ _____

Card Number _____ Exp. Date ___/___

Name on card: _____ Signature _____

Please make checks payable to Tiffany Harbor Productions.

Order Form

Telephone orders: Call 312-777-4002 ext. 7371

Fax orders: Dial 312-777-4002, followed by the Pause key twice, enter 7371, then press Send.

Mail orders: Build a Better Trade Show Image, Tiffany Harbor Productions, PO Box 901808, Kansas City, MO 64190–1808

Quantity Discounts:

1 - 24 books	No discount ($2495)
25 - 99 books	25% ($1875)
100 - 199 books	30% ($17.50)
200 - 299 books	40% ($15.00)

(Please call for pricing on quantities over 300, or books for resale.)

❑ Please send _____ copies of the book (ISBN #0-9712905-1-2).
I understand that I may return any books for a full refund,
no questions asked.

Subtotal $_____

Name: _____

Company Name: _____

Address: _____

City, State, Zip: _____

Phone: (____) _____

❑ Please subscribe me to the TradeShowTips Online newsletter,
free of charge, at this address: _____@_____

Sales tax: For Missouri addresses, please include 7.1% tax + $ _____

Shipping: $4.50 for the first book and
$1.50 for each additional book.   + $ _____

Payment: Please enclose payment with order.
Payment will be processed at time of shipment.   ——————
❑ Check   ❑ Money Order   ❑ MasterCard   ❑ VISA
Order Total $ _____

Card Number _____ Exp. Date ___/___

Name on card: _____ Signature _____

Please make checks payable to Tiffany Harbor Productions.